Your Inner Islands

The Keys to Intuitive Living

Will Tuttle, Ph.D.

Your Inner Islands: *The Keys to Intuitive Living*

2017 [2005] © Will & Madeleine Tuttle
Karuna Music & Art
1083 Vine Street
Healdsburg, CA 95448

Published by: Karuna Music & Art, www.willtuttle.com

Cover painting: Madeleine Tuttle

Art Garden Original Watercolor Paintings: Madeleine Tuttle (Viewable at www.willtuttle.com/Paintings.pdf; some books may include the paintings on a printed insert.)

Islands of Light Original Piano Music: Will Tuttle (Available through www.willtuttle.com and online music sources.)

The above music and art are created to accompany this book.

Printed in the United States of America

ISBN: 978-0-692-86540-8

Your Inner Islands

The Keys to Intuitive Living

Will Tuttle, Ph.D.

Islands of Light Song List

Compact Disc of Original Piano Music by Will Tuttle

1. Song of Understanding	3:22	Em, G
2. Dance of Light	3:30	B♭m, Gm
3. Song of B-flat	3:16	E♭
4. Song of Inner Spaces	3:20	Dm

Fantasia in F Major

5. Vivace	3:15	F
6. Tempestoso	3:32	Dm
7. Pastorale	2:52	F
8. Trionfale	4:14	F, D, F

Songs from an Art Garden

9. Lost Island	2:38	Em, G
10. Emerging Jewel	3:02	Em
11. Inner Doorway	3:22	Em
12. Time Beyond Time	4:08	Fm, Dm
13. Interbeing	3:09	G
14. The Arrival	2:57	F

15. Song of the Truth-Field	4:38	G
16. Dance of the Jeweled Web	3:40	Em, G
17. Song of Returning Home	4:21	C
18. Song of the Caring Earth	3:55	D

Table of Contents

Acknowledgments

This book, and the music and art that accompany it, constitute a multimedia course for developing the spiritual faculty of intuition, and I'd like to thank those who have helped bring it to fruition. This course has grown out of the classes, workshops, seminars, and retreats I've been facilitating over the past thirty years.

For six years, during and after my Ph.D. work at the University of California, Berkeley, I taught a variety of college courses in the San Francisco bay area in which I was able to present many of the ideas and exercises in this book, and I'd like to thank the students of those classes for their valuable input. In the years since then, traveling to cities across North America and worldwide to present lectures, concerts, and also workshops on developing intuition, I am grateful to the many participants who have shared their experiences and enthusiasm, and helped refine these ideas.

Thanks also to the academic as well as the spiritual teachers who have blessed my life and contributed to this course of study by their presence and teachings, particularly Joseph Axelrod, Donald Gilbert, Seo Kyungbo Sunim, and Kusan Sunim. Thanks to those who read through the manuscript and offered suggestions for improving it, especially Zach Shatz, Evelyn Casper, and Regan Forest.

Special acknowledgement to my caring spouse Madeleine for her heartful involvement in presenting the workshops and her paintings that are an integral part of this course on developing intuition.

A positive revolution in consciousness is struggling to be born, and appreciation goes to all the many midwives for your efforts.

The main text of this book was published as an eBook on the *Islands of Light* enhanced CD in 2005. This current version has been revised and updated.

March 2017

Prologue

Intuition and the Islands of Light

We have heard that islands of light lie within us. Sanctuaries of understanding, peace, and intuitive wisdom, these inner islands seem to beckon. Perhaps we can make a journey to discover and explore them and in so doing, develop within us keys to living more freely and creatively on this Earth.

What greater gift can we give to ourselves and to others than our sincere effort to cultivate our intuition? What could be more valuable than a reliable source of guidance in our daily lives that supports us in fulfilling the deepest yearnings of our heart and unfolding the highest potential within us for understanding and blessing our world?

Intuition is tuition from within. Unlike conventional rational forms of knowing that are based on dividing and comparing, and a basic separation between the knower and what is known, intuition seems to be inner and non-dual, and is associated with enhanced creativity, spirituality, and healing. When we intuit, we go "into it," and the "we" and the "it" merge in direct knowing. While rationality is outer and trackable, intuition flowers in inner silence and receptivity, and is neither objective nor linear. Nevertheless, it is empowering and beguiling, and stands beckoning at doorways that insistently call to us, an unrecognized and yet completely natural way of understanding that can provide valuable guidance on our spiritual path and in our everyday challenges and opportunities.

How do we cultivate intuition? What are the keys to intuitive living? Intuitive understandings are often best expressed through allegory. In this book we'll explore these questions by embarking on an allegorical adventure of discovery, using an ancient Buddhist metaphor for spiritual awakening, that of crossing. Enlightenment in this tradition is seen as a crossing from This Shore to the Other Shore. This Shore represents our current state of intuitive and spiritual development, and the Other Shore is our fully awakened potential, in which we become living expressions of the harmony, intuitive wisdom, and creative exuberance that are our potential, and that we can glimpse vaguely from This Shore.

Even though a seemingly vast ocean separates us from the Other Shore, there may be inner islands of inspiration and understanding that will assist and guide us as we make our crossing. It is thought that these islands exist beyond the horizon of our knowing. These fabled Islands of Light, also known as the Lost Islands, are said to be sanctuaries of revelation and spiritual power, and that they can be helpful connecting points on our journey toward the Other Shore. Each island, it is said, bears unique teachings and insights that can encourage another petal of our intuitive potential to unfold.

In addition to the language of words, which expresses ideas through allegory and verbal concepts, we will be using the languages of music and art as well, weaving words and music together throughout the journey of this book. The music is contained on the compact disc album, *Islands of Light*, (available from the author's website, and also available online on iTunes and other online sources). It includes eighteen pieces of original piano music composed and performed for this book by the author.

Reproductions of the watercolor paintings created by Madeleine Tuttle for the chapter entitled "Island of Imagination" are viewable at www.willtuttle.com/Paintings.pdf if not included as a separate color sheet at the back of the book.

Music and art have long been recognized as languages of intuition, and as our intuition opens, we seem to become better able to receive messages through their nonverbal rhythms, harmonies, melodies, and images. As we practice being receptive to the messages encoded in music and art, we can become more sensitive to the hidden connections between our inner and outer worlds. Opening to inspired music and art can feed our intuitive muse.

As we journey toward the Other Shore and search for the enigmatic Islands of Light, we are traveling within to places of more expanded and connected awareness. Perhaps we'll discover intuitive faculties that can help untangle, clarify, and illuminate our struggles and questions, and bring the peace of higher understanding to our hearts. Besides guiding us in our spiritual evolution, intuition may also be able to point the way to choosing wisely in our personal affairs, and to inspire us with fresh insights for our creative projects and inspiration for our daily lives. We may discover that we have no greater friend and ally than our intuition, and that this inner guidance can open us to higher levels of understanding and freedom. We recognize that our cultural upbringing has mostly ignored this valuable inner resource, and has failed to teach us how to cultivate intuition.

Perhaps the deepest yearning of all human beings, though we may often be distracted from remembering it, is to reach the Other Shore. This Other Shore has gone by a variety of names. In the Christian tradition, for example, it is said to be essential that we seek first the kingdom, and then everything shall be added unto us. This kingdom is understood to lie not outside of us, but to be within. The Other Shore is also said to likewise lie within us, as is the journey we make to reach it.

Our journey to reach the Other Shore is a journey from head to heart that can help to heal the divisions within us and to discover the inherent joy and blessedness of living. This is the adventure. The Other Shore, an undiscovered world, is calling.

We stand now on the deck of our ship, looking out over the harbor to the dark ocean stretching restlessly to the far horizon. The first island on the journey toward intuitive awakening is said to be the Island of Understanding, and it can perhaps reveal to intrepid pilgrims the right understanding that supports the rest of the voyage to the Other Shore. There are other legendary islands beyond the Island of Understanding that lie farther away, and we hope to reach those as well. Each island is said to be enchanted and filled with power, and to offer specific techniques and opportunities for discovering the keys to intuitive living.

Around us are the familiar sights and sounds of the harbor: the people fishing off the jetty, the gulls calling and flapping around us; the clanging of bells and buoys, the ruffling of sails, and the bubbling and roaring of motors as boats of many sizes and shapes maneuver over the choppy waters. Though we refer to ourself using the plural pronoun, this is a solo journey, and we are ready now to embark, alone, on this voyage.

Everything in our life has brought us to this point of departure, launching our ship on this journey of discovery. Behind us is our known world: the busy patterns that have held us for so long. Before us lies the immense and perilous ocean, and our journey to the Islands of Light and to the Other Shore beyond. The ocean reaches in here to this shallow port and to our docked ship, and waits restlessly, holding us while at the same time persistently beckoning. Something stirs within us and, no longer satisfied with the bustle of the harbor, we long for the freedom and challenge of adventure, to live more deeply and discover what treasures lie beyond the horizon of our small, known world. The Other Shore is calling.

Chapter 1

The Island of Understanding

As we sail out toward the deepening indigo waters, leaving the harbor, we feel a mixture of joy and sadness, excitement and trepidation. Looking back toward the clamor of the land receding behind us, we sense wistfully the possibility that we may not return here, and a hollow ache arises within us. We are leaving our world and the security it has given us.

Gliding over the waves toward the open ocean, the wind picks up, and our ship surges forward. Once we are well beyond the harbor, we begin to feel an unexpected sense of relief, as if old weights attached to our shoulders are falling away, lightening and freeing us. This feeling of relief builds, becoming an inexplicable gladness bursting in our heart as we look ahead over the trackless waters. Our sadness and trepidation lighten. We realize that whatever we have left behind, and whatever lies before us, right now we are following our heart's yearning, and there is enormous satisfaction in this. This moment is bright and real, delicious and timeless. We are alive! We savor the lift of every wave, every fragrant breath and sparkle of the sun. We can see for miles, and we spontaneously give thanks for this ship, this ocean, this life, and to everyone and every event that has brought us to this moment, bounding forward over the waves, traveling toward the Other Shore.

As the heaviness that we had gotten used to melts away, we feel our mind becoming clearer and our vision brighter. Old hurts and grudges arise, loosen, and peel away, blown far by the fresh wind that carries us forward. We send blessings to everyone we have ever known, thanking them all for contributing to this opportunity, and for the exhilaration and the potential of the voyage we are undertaking. We realize that even those of whom we have unsavory memories often played vital roles in bringing us to this adventure. We thank them all. There is no looking back. This open sea, splashing in the sun, is our destiny, and we sense that everything in our life has brought us to this moment. Perhaps there have been no mistakes, after all. Perhaps everything has been instrumental in bringing us here now. We can sense something within us dying, and something urging to be born.

Eventually we are out of sight of land, and we sail on for many days and nights. Searching the horizon, our eyes become tired and sometimes the winds oppose us or simply disappear. We do our best to continue on, even when the winds die down or whip the ocean waters into large and dangerous swells. At times the rain and wind lash us mercilessly, and we must work many sleepless hours just to keep afloat and on course.

The Islands of Light are uncharted, though we've heard they are somewhere to the southeast. For guidance, we rely on our compass and our inner sense. The first island, the Lost Island of Understanding, is said to be the hardest to reach, and we have heard it is only visible, to those allowed to see it, at dawn and at dusk.

After about three weeks of sailing, we are getting concerned because our water supply is starting to run low. Then one morning we notice that the light is somehow different, and that the air seems brighter. There is a sense of presence here, and so we sail very slowly and are especially watchful at dawn and at dusk. We find that by sitting quietly and listening within, letting go of thoughts and just being open, we can tune in to this sense of presence and we can notice when we are moving away from it, and when we are getting closer. We practice this meditative inner listening both day and night because we do not want to miss the mysterious island that we sense is lurking somewhere nearby.

As the days go by, our water supplies diminish further and though we realize that now we must return to land or risk facing dehydration, we continue patiently meditating and sailing slowly in the direction of our inner feelings. We feel how close we must be to the island. Sometimes we can hear a humming vibration, and occasionally see a shimmering brightness over the water. When we sail toward the brightness, the humming seems at times to increase.

We are becoming increasingly thirsty, however, and anxious. It seems we are being pushed to our utmost limits. The sun and moon revolve around us and we sail on, struggling to maintain our mental equilibrium as everything becomes increasingly dreamlike. Waking and dreaming drift into each other as we drift across waves of time and space that expand and contract bewilderingly. Our world becomes distressingly surreal.

A few more days pass and our water supply is almost exhausted. Then one night we dream of a great tree rooted in heaven and branching into the Earth, and awakening, we sit quietly on deck, searching the horizon all around us. The water is totally calm. Then, as the sun rises in the east, we see it! Shrouded in mist, off the starboard bow, we see the unmistakable shape of an island being caressed by the first rays of morning light. A deep thanksgiving fills us, and we utter a parched croak of joy. We allow ourselves to collapse onto the deck, our cracked lips smiling, and enjoy the release of tension, anxiety, and doubt. We realize that we are actually drifting toward the island, as if being pulled, and in a few hours, we are splashing through the water and walking onto dry land at last. Kneeling in the sand, thirsty and grateful, we rest a moment before exploring this beautiful place.

There are high hills here, and walking inland for several minutes, we come to a clear flowing stream with a deep pool. We drink and bathe and refresh ourselves. There are papaya trees as well, and we eat several of their delicious fruits, feeling invigorated and delighted at the abundance and beauty of the island.

Returning to the shore, we walk along the beach and eventually come upon a weathered wooden sign. On it are written these words:

> **The ox, trying to go through the gate, is stuck;**
> **Only his tail won't go through.**

We stop and sit down. There is a deep question in these two lines. What is it? What is this old wooden sign alluding to? An understanding begins to come to us, carried by the spirit of this Island of Understanding. We realize that these two lines are an old Zen *koan*.

We remember that in the Zen meditation tradition, a koan is a meditation question that is unanswerable by the rational mind. We see that as we contemplate the koan, our intuition is naturally stimulated and we feel the question is pushing us toward an understanding required to continue our journey. What is this koan pointing at? What is this ox? And what is the gate, and where does it lead? How could his little tail keep the ox from going through the gate? How absurd the image is! Why wouldn't his tail go through? What does it mean?

15

After a while, we consciously relax our mind as it probes this koan, chewing on it like it does every perceived problem, trying to solve it. Eventually we calm our mind enough to enter an inner quietness and then, mysteriously, we suddenly hear the presence of the island, as if speaking to us!

"Welcome. I am glad that you are here! I am called the Island of Understanding. It is not an easy journey to find me, and your perseverance has served you well. I am the first stop in your pilgrimage toward the Other Shore and I wish to help you deepen your understanding. But to acquire understanding, you need understanding! Don't let this worry you. Everything that your intuition discovers and understands is a paradox to your rational mind.

"Intuition is not an exotic gift, available only to rare and special people. Everyone is potentially intuitive, and deeply so. You would not have found me here without your intuition. Like the ox, you have passed the gate and entered the realm of intuition, which is your own true nature, but somehow, like the ox, you have a tail that won't allow you to go completely through. What is this tail? Why is it always with you, like the tail is always with the ox? Is it perhaps an old wound that accompanies you like a tail, not visible to your own eyes as it dangles behind you, an old nemesis that has you fooled into thinking it's your friend?"

The voice stops speaking and, instead, we begin to receive impressions as we keep our mind quiet and open. Tuning in to the wise presence of this island, we begin to realize that the ox's tail is an unrecognized assumption, always clinging to our conscious awareness. We gain a distinct impression of this assumption as an appendage, deep-rooted and strong. It is becoming clearer that this usually invisible assumption is an erroneous conviction that we are a thing and others are also things, and that as things we are fundamentally separate. We begin to see that the tail is a habit, and it is a virtually universal way of seeing: seeing others and oneself as distinct and basically competing objects. We see that this tail has been at the root of the inescapable sense of struggle we have always experienced.

We suddenly understand that the tail is also a tale as well. It relies on and feeds the old narrative our self tells itself, continually reinforcing our existence as a separate object. The mind, ever thinking and preoccupied with its personal story and with all the regrets, dramas, worries, and struggles that this story involves, becomes convinced that it is its tale. It steadfastly resists any inner state of silence and the clear awareness in which the tale stops because this seems like a death—the end of its existence. For the mind appendage that believes the story of its essential separateness, even a story of pain and sorrow is better than no story at all.

We see that the ox's tail is an old wound. Perhaps it is the wound of dualism, the deep sense that we are separate from the world. The tail's relentless narrative revolves around the mistaken assumption that it is a part separate from and at odds with others and the larger flow of life. The tail's tale keeps it firmly attached as an appendage to our awareness. How does it affect us? We see that in the culture in which we were raised, the assumption and the wound of separateness are so pervasive that the tail runs things and wags the ox . . . this tail will certainly get stuck in any gate.

"How is this wound finally healed?" we wonder. The island is back again, directly communicating with us.

"Perhaps the old, painful wound of separation is an illusion. Perhaps it is healed when you realize, directly and intuitively, that you have never been separate from the boundless source of your life. It seems that the conditioned mind will not be able to reach this understanding because it requires a certain leap in awareness, a radical and untrackable shift of perspective. Tears of joy and laughter may spill forth when you see it all directly. Perhaps the ox is free at every moment to enter the field of boundless freedom and joy.

When the ox, our true nature, understands clearly, his little tail can shrink back to its natural size. It has never actually been an obstruction! Your true nature may likewise be free to roam the fields of harmony and creativity once you understand the nature of the ox, and of your tail.

"Cultural programming, however, seems to make this understanding difficult to achieve. The deep belief in separateness is embedded in language, culture, and institutions, and it militates against intuition. From infancy, your training often reinforced the belief in separateness. You were taught to focus on the parts of everything, continually dividing in order to know. You were compelled to compartmentalize and fragment yourself, to compete with others, and to repress your innate capacities, intelligence, and empathy. Now you seem to be awakening and are beginning to recognize that much of the pervasive cultural programming is a wound inflicted by well-meaning parents, teachers, doctors, and others who were similarly wounded, and that as you question this indoctrination, you can liberate your mind.

"Whereas rationality is knowing by *dividing* (Greek: *ana-lysis*: "to break up") and *comparing* (from Latin *ratio*), nonrational intuition is direct knowing by relaxing, expanding, opening, and leaping to grander, more inclusive perspectives. At its fullest flowering, intuition can perhaps dissolve the old dichotomy between knower and known into a transcendent awareness that can lead to deeper insights, beyond the level of rationality and conditioned thinking.

"On this Island of Understanding, you have the opportunity to deepen your understanding, and to question, and realize that perhaps your human evolution is calling you to respect and explore intuition. Through this exploration, your tail, the belief that you are a separate thing, may begin to shrink to its proper size. This may be the way to heal the deep wound that gives rise to fear, craving, anger, greed, anxiety, and all the rest."

The island both reassures and challenges us: "Your old wound, the persistent illusion of a separate self, can be healed. This may be a key to opening the intuitive gate. The practice of meditation can be helpful, and there is nothing exotic about it. The old saying is that meditation is not what you think. It is the art of witnessing the continuous inner monologue of thinking and internal storytelling that feeds the tale of separateness and that may be keeping you divided, distracted, and self-absorbed.

"Meditation can be nourished by understanding that concepts, by themselves, can never deliver wisdom. They can be valuable if they bring you to the edge of themselves, to the cliff, as it were, beyond which they cannot take you. Then you are called to let go, and this letting go into the awareness beyond concepts is meditation. When you practice meditation, and practice letting go of clinging to the known, you are taking responsibility for your awakening.

"Meditation may be understood as inner listening, a relaxed alertness and openness that help you travel outside the boundaries of your experience and enter the universal. Through the practice of meditation, you may metaphorically pass through the gate and enter the field of liberation."

We continue to explore this breathtaking island, contemplating the ideas we have encountered here, and the koan of the ox's tail. We stop and rest, sitting under a tree. We notice a squirrel sitting on a branch of the tree, eating a nut. Contemplating the scene, we note that the conditioned mind sees separation, the squirrel and tree definitely separate and distinct entities with different goals and agendas. This way of seeing, as it looks more acutely, seems to contract and see conflict and competition. The squirrel is competing with other squirrels for the tree's nuts, and the tree's goal seems to be in conflict with the squirrel, for it can never reproduce itself if squirrels eat all of its nuts. This is all true and provable to our conditioned mind, and we allow ourselves to consciously experience this way of seeing for a few minutes.

Now we relax and open, and let go of thinking. We practice looking as the island has suggested, with the mind of intuition. We sense interconnectedness, and see the fundamental cooperation between these two beings, the tree and the squirrel. One provides oxygen, housing, food, shade, and support, and the other provides carbon dioxide, fertilizer, and a means to spread seeds about. More deeply, we see how each provides a context for the other, one offering stability and one mobility, and how they share giving and receiving, and energy and humor, among other things.

Even on a purely physical level, the cells of the tree become cells of the squirrel, and the cells of the squirrel become cells of the tree. We realize further that they are parts of a community which they serve and which serves them, and that they are each fulfilling their roles in this community, and expressing the wisdom of this community which, as we continue opening, becomes larger and larger, including the island, the ocean, the Earth, the sun and sky and, expanding beyond one boundary after another, revealing a glimpse of the interconnectedness of all levels and expressions of being.

As we continue to practice looking more deeply, we see that the apparently separate things we call "tree" and "squirrel" may not be fundamentally separate. With this understanding, we as the perceiver are also drawn into the ever-deepening awareness that we are no longer a separate observer. We sense there are actually no "things" at all. As the wall of "me" dissolves in these waves of understanding, "squirrel," "tree," and "me" can begin to be seen more clearly as manifestations of and within an unimaginably vast presence that is beyond naming. We are sensing the island's teachings, and how words and concepts can limit our awareness, and how pronouns and nouns can become distortions that distance us and distract us from awareness of the deeper process unfolding around and within us. We get a glimpse of this freedom from compulsive thinking and how this may help us develop intuition.

Now the squirrel runs through the grass and up another tree. Is that what is really happening? Where is "squirrel"? Where is "tree"? Where is "me"? Are these separate objects or are they mental categories and verbal constructions? Intuition smiles with the delight of being present and opening to vistas of interconnectedness. This kind of seeing for some reason seems more accessible here on this island than in the culture we left behind.

The island speaks to us again: "Intuition is perhaps the higher knowing that fulfills rational thinking. Like rationality, intuition can be educated, trained, and developed. The way is through practice, as with any art or craft. Unfortunately, in school, you were trained mainly in taking things apart in order to understand them. Now you are aware in ways you couldn't be as a child, and yearn to reclaim the neglected and repressed intuition to help put your world back together again.

"Without intuition can you understand directly the deep interconnectedness and sacredness of life? Can you experience joy, beauty, or compassion? Without intuition, can you put back together what you have taken apart? Can you and your culture avoid insanity? This is the tragedy of your people, and the source of your mission. You have perhaps been called to bring healing to your wounded culture. This may mean healing it first within yourself.

"Remember when you were a child in school and the teacher would ask the class questions. You learned in an impactful way that there were 'right' and 'wrong' answers to the teacher's questions. You were injected with a paradigm, the underlying narrative of your culture, and it was impactful because you saw directly that getting 'wrong' answers led to disapproval, bad grades, trouble at home, and rejection, and being 'right' led to success, approval, power, and safety. Right and wrong, the old wound of dualism, got its claws in early and deep. As a child, you were like a sponge, soaking up the cues from your culture so that, small and vulnerable, you could survive and make sense of things here.

"Thinking back, weren't you continually drilled in seeking right and avoiding wrong? Weren't you compelled to wear the approved cultural lenses for taking things apart? For dominating and excluding? It seems that enforced concepts of right and wrong are effective for this. Further, as you sought dutifully for the right answers in school, and raised your hand and managed occasionally to give the right answer, sometimes you would hear, 'Very good! How do you *know* that's the right answer?' Scary question! You learned there were basically two types of responses to this. One was, 'I see it right here on page 79 of the book.' 'Yes, class, very good! See, it's on page 79 here,' the teacher would say. So you were trained to accept *outside* authority for what is right. The Book contains The Truth, you were told in school, and you had to accept these cultural assumptions of rightness or your very *survival* was, in your young mind, threatened.

"The other valid response to the teacher's question, 'How do you know your answer is right?' was to give a logical, trackable, linear sequence of thinking to support your answer. This demand for linear rationality pervaded history and geography as much as mathematics. From early in your schooling, the basic interconnectedness of knowledge was ignored as it was divided into categories and subjects. You learned that The Book—outside authority—and logical positivist thinking were the *only* safe guarantors of validity. You learned it at school, at church, and at home; it was the invisible cultural air everyone breathed. If you had responded when asked at age eight the great epistemological question, 'How do you know if what you say is true is actually true?' with: 'I know it's true, teacher, but I don't know *how* I know exactly. I just have a feeling;' or, 'The answer came from the silence within myself, from an inner knowing.' 'Wrong! That is *not* good!'

"As a participant in your culture, you were likely compelled to practice many attitudes that inhibit intuition. Now, maturing in understanding, you realize that what was right for one generation may no longer serve another. Perhaps most of what you learned to be true or right in school and from the media was often severely distorted, especially from a perspective based on intuitive values rather than material values. So as you continue your life adventure of learning, and your quest to reach the Other Shore, it may be helpful to recognize and acknowledge the enormous amount of practice you have devoted since childhood to becoming proficient in dualistic thinking, in separating things, and in looking *outside* yourself for the truth."

The breeze plays quietly with the palm fronds above us. It is unsettling to be told that our training in the system we were born into is such an impediment to the higher knowing that we are seeking.

"Here on the Island of Understanding, you may be realizing that intuition requires training and practice, and this practice seems to be, in many ways, in a direction opposite from your earlier practice. You may find it helpful now to learn to look *inside* for the truth, and learn to *suspend* habitual judgment of right and wrong in order to see more clearly what is happening, and the interconnections. You may like to learn to *relax* and *expand* rather than contract, to let go of verbal thinking as the *source* of knowing, to let go of the compulsive orientation to past and future, and to cultivate your intuition and imagination. None of these is easy, given your prior training, and yet your efforts to develop intuition may help bring peace, healing, and joy into your life and into your world.

"As you know in your bones, your culture is in many ways based on asserting power *over* others and nature. You may see that you learned as a child that this is right and acceptable in countless subtle ways. Perhaps it was right there on your dinner plate every day, a slaughtered, commodified animal, and perhaps you were even compelled to eat it. Separatistic thinking is a tool that seems to serve this orientation of domination. It may be coming clearer to you why you have been trained in analysis, competition and compartmentalization, and why intuition, which connects and looks deeply, has been ignored and suppressed. Since intelligence includes the ability to make meaningful connections, the higher intelligence of your culture may actually be shrinking amid the glut of information. Is information that is disconnected from the meaning and wisdom that intuitive knowing provides actually helpful, or does it create more confusion and opportunity for domination and exploitation? The shrinking of your culture's higher intelligence may however be profitable for an elite that seeks to control you and your institutions, but is anyone actually happier for it?

"We can perhaps begin to understand that we humans develop through stages, from pre-rational stages of understanding to rational and then on to post-rational or transrational stages of understanding. These latter modes of understanding, termed intuitive, can contain and make use of rationality, but don't seem to be limited or bound by it. Intuition can be seen to be a higher evolutionary stage. Rationality is certainly a useful tool, within its proper context, and can serve the higher understanding intuition provides.

"By now, many of you in the postmodern West seem to be aware that the usual ways of thinking and behaving create more stress, more waste, more misery, and less meaning and fewer resources for effectively solving the problems you're facing. Perhaps developing intuition is one of the next cultural imperatives for your society, and you are, perhaps, a delegate sent by the deep yearning of your people for healing. You may be their emissary and the urge within you that has propelled you here may be more than just yours alone.

"It is becoming increasingly obvious, at least to some, that dualistic conventional thinking can no longer properly serve even that bastion of rationalism, science. Physics, being the most physical and mathematically-based of the sciences, was, as you know, the first to hit the wall, when the either/or dualism of the scientific method could no longer explain the basic nature of reality: light is not *either* a particle *or* a wave, it is *both, and* what it appears to be depends entirely on the observer. That realization ushered in the slow and painful fall of the hallowed "objective observer" myth that was one of the assumptions of scientism, the view that positivist science is the only authentic means to truth. This objective observer notion seems to be the ox's tail dressed up in a scientist's white jacket, measuring and attempting to know a reality it conceives to be essentially separate from itself. On this Island of Understanding, such postures can only strike the intuitive mind as somewhat comical. Perhaps scientists are indeed part of their own experiments."

On this Island of Understanding, we can literally feel our mind expanding, and it is not always comfortable. As our capacities are stretched, many of the familiar and comfortable handholds on reality are being questioned. We can vaguely sense that much of our thinking has been narrow, rigid, and self-preoccupied. How do we proceed?

The spirit of the island continues: "Perhaps the way to do this is through practice. To become a knitter, you knit; a dancer, you dance; a painter, you paint; but to become more intuitive, what do you practice? Perhaps practicing meditation is one of the roads to intuitive knowing.

"This island is quiet. Meditation and inner listening are easier here. You may discover during your stay here that the practice of meditation contains its own reward and is, in and of itself, a deeply fulfilling 'activity.' Non-activity is probably a better word. You may discover that the effects of regularly practicing meditative inner listening and witnessing ripple out into every aspect of your life. It may help free you from the domination of culturally conditioned thinking and to connect with your intuition. Every hour of the day can be an opportunity to discover more of the inner terrain that lies unexplored within you. You may discover there are many benefits to diligently training your attention.

"For example, a person fluid and comfortable with a musical instrument, enjoying the unfolding of rhythms and melodies while improvising, and carried away on the wings of the Muses, perhaps filling the hearts of an audience with soaring joy, has spent countless hours practicing with that instrument to free the spirit of music within for outer expression. Just so, as you practice meditation, returning your attention repeatedly to this present moment, you may be slowly giving birth to mental clarity, to emotional richness and equanimity, and to the creative freedom and spiritual maturity that can help reveal the beauty of life to you. You may also find you become more understanding and caring of others as your perspective widens and as you learn to watch your mind with awareness, rather than being swept along with all the thoughts and reactions of the ceaseless inner dialog. The practice of meditation trains attention, returning it persistently to alert awareness in this present moment."

In the uncanny silence that permeates this Island of Understanding, we begin to see and experience things in new ways. Days pass, and we find that we increasingly sense that we are not merely a concrete object arising and passing away in time. Looking out over the mysterious ocean one afternoon, we feel ourselves energized and related to the scene before us. The vividness increases and suddenly we hear the waves as if within us, and feel the breeze inside us, and hear the far away laugh of a gull inside us as well. The sun shines within us, and everything seems to be happening inside what we are, not outside us as we are accustomed.

Slowly the experience fades, and we feel the island's now familiar benevolent presence lapping at the edge of our consciousness, capturing our attention: "Ah! Very good. This way of seeing may help fuel your journey home to the Other Shore. The world, though seeming to be outside you, may more accurately be understood to arise within what you are, which is consciousness. As your intuition develops, you may discover greater harmony in your life as you understand more clearly your unity with the world around you and with your source. Your relationships, your work, your eating habits, your patterns of consumption may become more aligned with compassion as the realization deepens that harming and confining others always harms and confines you, and the more you free others, the freer you will be.

"Compassion and intuition seem to feed each other, like the paradoxical growth of a tree's roots and branches. Which causes which? We cannot say, for without the roots deepening, the branches could not grow, and without the branches growing, the roots could not go deeper! If each would wait for the other to grow first, maybe they would both wait forever and there would be no growth. Perhaps they are not actually separate, like intuition and compassion are not fundamentally separate. To understand them we are called to see the greater whole that they serve and that serves them: the *tree* is growing. It is a process without separate parts; if we divide it up, perhaps it is only because we are divided."

These words reverberate within us and we look out over the waves below us, pondering them. Each wave is unique, each wave is born, lives awhile, and eventually dies on the inevitable shore, and yet each wave *is* the eternal ocean. The ocean itself gives rise to countless waves, and is in, and is, each wave, and yet it seems that no individual wave can grasp the totality of its true nature, the ocean, without leaving the confines of its narrow wave perspective and realizing that it and all waves have the same source, the ocean. They do not actually die. What they are is the eternal ocean; they are not merely fleeting waves.

As we watch the lines of waves endlessly rising, surging forward, curling, and crashing on the beach, we practice seeing the two levels of truth simultaneously: that every wave is a unique individual, and that it is all just the ocean happening. After a while, our eyes take in the palm trees lining the beach below, reaching toward the sun and holding onto the Earth, and we find we can see them also as waves, also arising and passing, manifestations of a greater ocean that is less obviously seen.

The island returns again, like a gentle and wise elder, continuing, "What you are seeing may be significant. Waves are created of the ocean itself, and perhaps when you see this directly about yourself and all life, you can sense the source within you. For some people, this can be a form of prayer. It can become a communion that transcends dualism. For the wave, prayer is the process of intuitively understanding that its true nature is the ocean. For you, it is similar.

"Intuition seems to be both the treasure behind the locked door, and, ironically, the key that opens that door as well. It is the treasure because it confers wisdom, healing, spiritual awakening, creative exuberance, freedom, and joy. It's the key because it lights the pathway to the door. It's intuition because it takes place outside the territory of a separate self-concept, beyond the programmed thinking of the mind. If your intuitive eyes continue to open, perhaps they will be able to sense the deeper connections between events that are invisible to most. Maybe there are *only* events, actually, for what are selves and objects but events arising and passing in time? Perhaps there are no self-existing things anywhere, except in the concepts of the thinking, concretizing mind. Perhaps with this understanding, freedom can be born—and perhaps the ox's tail will deflate. I've heard that the grass in the field is sweet and fresh!

"The old saying is that 'there is no way to peace, peace is the way.' Perhaps the path and the goal are one, unfolding together continually. It seems that the barren knowing of disconnected thinking produces but a garden of knives, fences, cages, and dangerous weapons; and it seems that watered by intuition, soft and radiant flowers begin to emerge and dance. I invite you to cultivate this garden, which is your true home, your own mind. I invite you to bring your attention regularly to touch this present moment.

"Take a breath, and expel it slowly. Can you feel yourself present in your body, feel the weight and physicality of this experience? Notice the smells and sounds and visual arisings, the temperature, the air, and the sky. Without thinking, simply be, just for this brief moment. Aware. Just this. Here. Just now. Simply being. Nothing but this. Awake. Present…

"Meditation, even if practiced for only a short time, seems to be like a breeze that freshens, a cool wave that opens up your eyes and ears and feelings. Practicing regularly, your life becomes the practice of awareness. I invite you to explore this path to awakening and freedom, this path of intuition. Maybe the ox's tail will shrink back to size and the ox, your true nature, will stroll through the gate to enjoy his boundless life. As you deepen your roots of awareness, perhaps your branches of intuition will automatically unfold higher toward heaven. Perhaps you are a tree. And perhaps you'll find the ox's tail."

The island's words flow to us like an inner stream, dissolving old knots and tensions. Confusions and complications melt away and dilemmas evaporate as we sit quietly in the presence that saturates the atmosphere of this island.

We stay on the island for another several weeks, walking, swimming, resting, practicing inner listening, and allowing the island's wisdom to penetrate us more fully. Several more times we experience the sense of stretching and expanding, and perceive the world as arising inside of us. Grateful for the gifts of understanding the island has bestowed, we eventually feel the Other Shore calling us on.

An inner window has opened in our mind, revealing the beginning outlines of a new understanding of our nature and of the false tale of separateness. We sense the bright field of freedom that lies beyond the gate of the little tail and outside the prison of programmed self-preoccupation, and how it shines beyond the confines of discursive thinking.

The ox of our true self smells the field of joy and freedom that are his home and realizes there is nothing in his way but his little tail. His nostrils flare; his eyes are bright! His great heart leaps! How delicious this moment is! Palm trees flutter in the cool morning breeze, and far away and within, we hear the call of a gull. As we walk the beach, saying good-bye to the island and thanking her, we realize that the old wooden sign has disappeared. The koan is within us now.

Before we leave the island, we sit quietly and hear her message to us as music swirling over the sea and through her trees. We listen deeply, and through the rhythm, melodies, and harmony of the music, receive understanding that goes beyond what words can capture.

(For a little taste of this music, please listen to "Song of Understanding," piece number one on the accompanying album, *Islands of Light*.)

Chapter 2

The Island of Energy

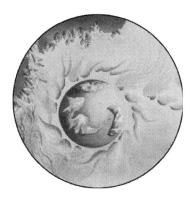

It is hard to leave the beauty and abundance of the Island of Understanding, but as we watch the island receding behind us to the west, we thank her for all she has shown and given us. We sense the island as a wise grandmother, and her guidance telling us to continue sailing eastward, and that by practicing her teachings, we will reach the next island safely. We have fresh supplies of water, bananas, papaya, and coconuts, and a strong breeze from the southwest. The ocean carries us along like one of her waves.

After several weeks of sailing, we encounter a violent tropical storm. Heavy clouds dump sheets of rain upon us, and roaring winds stir the water into huge swells that threaten to swamp us as they toss us about like a little toy. It takes all our energy to keep the ship from capsizing, and when the waves get especially high and begin to pour across the deck and there is little we can do but pray, we remember the teachings of the Island of Understanding, that the waves and the ocean are one.

Soaked and clinging to our heaving vessel, our prayer is remembering the truth that all being is a manifestation of the infinite source. We focus on this understanding. We, as waves, are expressions of the same ocean that is the source of these outer waves and of all life, and our prayer is affirming this in our consciousness and also giving thanks that every event is a manifestation of this living ocean. Focusing on the essential and abiding peace that we sense shines hidden within the outer appearance of the storm, we endeavor to relax and trust the loving presence that we feel.

The ship continues to be thrown about, and we hold to the teaching that the Island of Understanding shared with us, making a conscious effort to open to the understanding that we are essentially eternal and undamageable because our source has these same qualities. We are never separate from this source. We are a wave; we are the ocean. Our prayer is an effort to question and disregard the testimony of our outer senses, and instead to cultivate our awareness that we are an expression of eternal consciousness. When thoughts of fear arise, we do our best to replace them with this understanding. As this awareness gradually grows in us, we begin to relax and eventually we drift into sleep, rocked by the ocean's giant hand in great arcing swells through time, space, and dreams.

The morning sunlight urges our eyelids open; we smile, looking into the clear sky shining serenely over our gently rocking ship. To the south of the sun, we see mist and a sense of brightness. Sailing slowly toward it, we begin to see the distinct outlines of land on the horizon. By mid-afternoon, we can see a lofty volcano in the distance, and before long we are drawing close to a spectacularly beautiful island.

Black sand beaches glisten before lush tropical forests that climb up the sides of the mountain. We anchor in an inlet where a stream tumbles over a cliff into the salty blue-green water, and soon we are walking the beach. There is a sense of power here, blended with a palpable sense of benevolence, and it turns our walk first into a euphoric stroll and then into a delightful spontaneous dance. The energy is so strong here, like music, that we just let it move us, and follow its promptings. Sometimes spinning and whirling, and then softly swaying, we play on the beach, and are played by invisible musical strings that ride the warm island breeze.

(For a sense of the music we hear on this island beach, please listen to piece number two, "Dance of Light," on the accompanying album, *Islands of Light*.)

Our dancing slows eventually, and we feel the music entering into our body as energy, running in channels up and down, tingling and vibrating. The energy moves through us, and we feel our body expanding as the energy fills us, purifying and washing through us. Slowly we begin to see images, like shadows, emerging before us on the beach. As we become aware of vibrating at increasingly higher frequencies, we hear a humming sound, and the shadow images begin to glow; as we expand more, we realize that these glowing images are bright beings who have been here all along. The island seems to be raising our vibration so we can perceive them. This seems to make the splendor surrounding us even more stunning.

One of the beings, appearing as a friendly old gentleman, glides over and begins communicating with us using only thought, welcoming us to the island. We hear this, as a communication from within:

"There may be much more than meets the physical eye. Perhaps you can only see, and always see, what you are energetically prepared to see. Perhaps you can only feel, hear, and think what you're energetically prepared to feel and hear and think. Maybe it would be helpful to learn how to raise the level of your energy. Otherwise, you may be like a person who lives in a beautiful and grand mansion but wanders around in the dim light of the basement and never finds the stairs that lead to the mansion's splendid views and treasure-rooms. With a little practice you can perhaps learn to raise your energy higher, and with more practice, higher still.

"One good way to raise your energy is through cultivating inner receptivity through prayer and meditation. You'll learn more about these things later. There are, however, other important elements to raising your energy that you might like to understand. You probably won't be able to meditate or pray effectively unless your energy level supports it.

"It's helpful to understand that you have been conditioned by your culture's intensely materialistic orientation, in which matter is seen as primary and self-existent. This materialism distorts and limits understanding because it blinds people to the essential primacy of energy and consciousness. These are much more difficult to quantify than matter and have been ignored when possible, or seen as derivative from matter. The conventional understanding in science, for example, has been that matter is primary and that energy, like heat and light from the sun, manifests from matter, and that consciousness, like the human brain, evolves from matter.

"The new frontier of understanding in your culture seems to be that consciousness is primary, and gives rise to and conditions energy and matter. Elevating consciousness seems to be the key to elevating your level of energy and to transforming negative perceptions and emotions, bringing healing and joy to the physical body and world. The most elevated form of consciousness is love, and all beings, planets and suns may be manifestations of this consciousness. Opening to this understanding is a form of prayer. Yesterday, you remembered this truth: that the ocean, the wind and waves, and you and your ship all arise from and are reflections of eternal consciousness, and this changed your perception, and through this prayer of understanding, you planted a seed, which is bearing fruit right now, as your safe arrival here with us. On this Island of Energy, you can understand that all experience arises in consciousness, like your dreams when sleeping. This may be a key to developing your intuition.

"When you see the light of the sun, you are seeing consciousness, and when you feel his warmth, you are feeling consciousness. When you see, or feel, or hear anything at all, it is consciousness that makes it possible. That you perceive intelligence and consciousness as visible light, for example, may be due to the particular way your body-mind selectively receives and interprets conscious energy. Your sense organs not only allow perception, they may also narrowly define what range of possibilities you will be able to see, hear, feel, smell, think about, and so forth. Where does it all happen? Within consciousness only!

"Perhaps, for example, you do not need physical eyes to see. Perhaps seeing is actually an attribute of consciousness, and what you are able to see depends on the quality of your consciousness. Physical matter itself has no ability to see or hear or think. It is actually consciousness that sees, perceives, and conceives. We seemed to be invisible to you when your level of energy was too low to see us, but your energy was nevertheless high enough to sense our presence, and you found yourself dancing with delight on this seemingly uninhabited beach. To help you understand and see us, we fed our consciousness to you, which you felt as becoming more energized. You could feel your energy rising. You still seem to need our help. If we stop sending our consciousness to you, what happens?"

He and the other glowing presences begin to fade and disappear.

"To help you understand more clearly, with your permission, we will raise your energy level briefly to illustrate. Please sit down comfortably here on the sand."

We do so, and soon begin to hear a humming sound similar to what we heard earlier as he reappears with the others. The pitch of the humming rises higher, though, and we feel our body expanding. The light beings become larger and more dazzling, slowly merging into a brilliant radiance before us. We feel our body vibrating as the humming goes higher and then is joined by a deep roaring sound, and the exhilarating pressure of expansion becomes almost unbearable. Suddenly we burst through a seeming bubble and the pressure is instantly released. The light becomes waves of dazzling radiance, and we hear music, beautiful and uplifting. We *are* the radiance, and the music and the space containing it all. Aware and boundless. Rainbow webs and filaments of light merge, dance, and disappear. Freedom and joy flood through us. Pure timeless being without limits, without boundaries, without a center or fringe, without self. Just openness and light....

We suddenly wonder what we look like now, and with this thought, the light and music fade away and we become aware that we are sitting on the beach in the evening light. We feel euphoric, yet strangely hollow inside, like a shell filled with nothing but space and light, and like we've been washed inside with liquid light. Soon the radiant gentleman has reappeared before us, smiling. We notice that our thrilling experience, so real while it was occurring, now has the feeling of a dream. Again, as if from within, we hear these words:

"Yes, though it may now feel like a dream, what you saw and felt may be more real than anything you take as real from your physical senses. We assisted you in raising your energy beyond the usual level of self-consciousness. We did not impose anything, but joined with you to reveal your boundlessness to yourself. As your consciousness transcended old limits, you felt as if you might burst. You can learn to do this on your own, as you learn to raise your energy. Your years of effort and seeking have brought you to us, and our time together here is the consequent opportunity, and there is more to come. With your permission, we would like share with you now some practical ways to raise and maintain your energy at the levels necessary for wisdom and insight.

"One helpful way to increase your energy is to consciously cultivate kindness and respect in your relationships with other living beings and even with seemingly inanimate objects. This you can begin today and every day, and practice diligently. As you send positive and loving energy to everyone and into every situation, you help raise both your own and others' energy and create the conditions for healing and transformation. Judgment and criticism of others, even when unspoken, actually reinforces whatever you are condemning in others because of the interconnectedness of consciousness. Your negative views of others thus do them a disservice, and your expectations tend to be fulfilled because your consciousness manifests not only your dreams at night, but your experiences while waking as well. You may be more telepathic with others than you realize. As your energy level increases, the field of love and appreciation that you radiate will naturally develop and become a field of freedom emanating from you that may encourage others to question their limiting assumptions and help them fulfill higher potentials.

"It's helpful to be aware of the general tone of your feelings. A sense of thankfulness, of sympathetic joy, and of calm peacefulness are signs that your energy is high, and these are the inner states that build energy as well. Frustration, self-concern, condemnation, anxiety, and trying to impress others and fulfill their expectations are all indications of lowered energy, and they also drain energy. Finding and embodying your uniqueness, beyond the dictates of family, social conditioning, peer pressure, and old childhood wounding, may help raise your awareness and energy significantly.

"There seem to be many practices that can help to raise and purify your energy. For example, in the morning, when you awaken, you may find it helpful to fill your first thoughts with gratitude. You can practice giving thanks for the precious opportunity of another day and the many possibilities for greater wisdom, abundance, love, and creative expression that can be discovered and cultivated today. Your source is boundless. As you cultivate these thoughts, you may like to notice and acknowledge any inner resistance. With increased energy, this sense of gratitude will become more spontaneous.

"You may also find that working directly with energy is helpful, and a regular practice of meditation can support more active ways of generating and balancing energy through Tai Chi, Qi Gong, yoga, reiki, or other disciplines. As you know, the energy we have been referring to has gone by many names, such as *chi, ki, prana,* orgone energy, *élan vital,* inner light, the Force, the Holy Spirit, the golden elixir, and there are many paths that cultivate it.

"Yoga, stretching, and Tai Chi initiate greater flexibility in mind and body, allowing more energy to flow through the energy channels of your body-mind. Qi Gong can be a way to manage and generate energy. Dance, gymnastics, aerobic exercise, weight training, and martial arts can all build energy levels. They can be effective especially if practiced regularly and meditatively without self-centered motives. Cultivating the awareness that you are an expression of consciousness, rather than identifying with a material form, accelerates all of these practices, and may eventually replace them.

"Nature may be another helpful ally in raising energy. You may find it helpful to take time daily to connect with nature in a way that is meaningful and nurturing for you. You can find ways to deepen your connection with the tranquility and beauty of the natural world, leaving behind the world of machines and human constructions for a while. You can learn to notice nuances in nature, to greet the many colorations of the sky, to honor the various animals you encounter, and appreciate the forests, rivers, mountains, shorelines, and deserts you visit. You'll naturally yearn to minimize your negative impact on the natural world, leaving no physical trace, if possible, that you have been there. As you become more comfortable in nature, you'll naturally yearn to refrain from and prevent actions that disturb or harm animals or ecosystems.

"The water in rivers, streams, lakes, and oceans can cleanse and refresh your energy field. Baptizing yourself daily in natural water, your spirit will be renewed. Perhaps you can bare your feet to touch the Earth, the forest floor or sandy beach, and feel the energy of the Earth rejuvenating your body.

"We invite you to walk, dance, dream, and wander in the beauty of forests, mountains, and ocean beaches. Drinking in the sun, the moon, the kinship of trees and shrubs, and the good tidings of breezes, birds, and wildflowers, you may find renewed energy, and a cleansing of your being. Spending several days in nature, without worldly distractions, will increase your energy significantly; you may find that solitary time in nature is particularly healing and effective.

"Opening to the ancient rhythms of the Earth, stars, and seasons may attune you to your heart's wishes and strengthen your spiritual roots. You may find that when you return to the world, you carry more energy, and that you understand and feel the dissonance of modern culture more acutely. Sensitized and purified, it will perhaps be sad to realize how far from the harmony of organic shapes and sounds your culture has strayed in its cities, factories, and mechanized farms. When you open to nature as a student, guest, and loving friend, you may find that you return strengthened, revitalized, and spiritually nourished.

"Your posture and your breathing can also be keys to increasing energy. Whether walking, sitting, or standing, you may find it helpful to be conscious of your posture so that your spine is straight, relaxed, and balanced, and your head rests gently above your shoulders, and is not protruding forward, stressing your neck. Allowing your breath to be deep and fill the lowest part of your lungs, and breathing only through your nose, you'll find you're most effectively absorbing the energy in the air.

"It seems that when our posture is lofty, our lower belly naturally relaxes, allowing our breathing to become deep and relaxed, vitalizing our body-temple with energy. Then our center of gravity naturally drops down from where it is in most ordinary people, the head and neck area, to the area just below the navel, *the dan-t'ien* as it is referred to in some systems of energy cultivation. Practicing this, you may find yourself becoming more intuitive and centered, shifting out of your head and coming more consciously into your heart and solar plexus and belly. We invite you to practice allowing yourself to move through your day with the belly as your center, breathing deeply and calmly. With practice, you may find that you have abundant energy for every undertaking, and that you naturally become a dancer and poet as you flow through daily life.

"We also invite you to take time to stretch and breathe deeply, to smile often and notice the details around you with relaxed and appreciative eyes. You may find it helpful to do a few cleansing breaths in the morning: just exhale every bit of air from your lungs by powerfully contracting your diaphragm and abdominal muscles, completely clearing out the old stale air from your lungs, and inhale deeply, repeating several times.

"Standing for a minute or two and imagining you are a tree can be a simple and effective way to build energy and feel more grounded. Imagining you're a favorite type of tree, with every exhalation, feel and visualize your roots going more deeply into the Earth. With every inhalation, feel and visualize the enriching, invigorating energy of the Earth flowing from your roots up through the soles of your feet, and filling the entire trunk and being of the tree that you are. With renewed energy, exhale again, sending your roots even deeper into the Earth, and allow your next inhalation to draw even more energy up into your trunk and into every cell of your being. Allow the energy to build within you, and your feeling of being rooted deeply into the Earth to grow strong while you repeat this several more times, or for as long as you'd like.

"Next, allow your arms to float up and imagine they are branches reaching up into the sky. With every exhalation, imagine your limbs reaching higher into the sky, spreading more branches, twigs, and leaves from your fingertips. On the inhalation, imagine and feel the energy of the cosmos entering through your leaves and branches, and filling your entire being. This energy allows you on your next exhalation to send your branches higher into the sky, allowing more energy to flow into you through your leaves and branches from the universe. Keep breathing, letting the energy build within you, and feeling yourself connected with the sky and all that it represents. You can open to the energy of the sun and moon, the stars and galaxies, the clouds, wind, birds, and rain. Entering into the joy of being a tree, bridging heaven and Earth, you can feel yourself being rooted in both heaven and Earth, and partaking of both.

"Finally, you can allow your arms to come back down and continue feeling your connection with the Earth and with the sky. Your posture will be naturally erect and poised, and your breathing will flow in a relaxed way deeply into the floor of your abdomen. When you move about now, you may like to be aware of your center in your abdominal area and move from there, a walking bridge between heaven and Earth, spirit and matter. The idea is to relax, smile, watch, listen, and be open. A quiet walk in nature can now be a delight, every sense open to the wonder of being present to the magnificence of the natural world.

"There are many other ways to increase energy. Dancing whatever energy is manifesting in the moment can be healing and uplifting, as can simply opening to the energy field of nature, perhaps under a tree or by water. A partner can 'bathe' you in energy with his or her hands or just by being present. Embracing large trees and connecting with their energy field through your hands are ancient ways of building, exchanging, and purifying energy. Countless techniques, practices, visualizations, postures, and attitudes that contribute to increasing energy have been discovered and shared, openly or secretly, in virtually every culture since time immemorial. All these ways are part of your human heritage, and according to your interest and inner potential, you may be led to discover and learn particular ones.

"The foods you eat can either raise or drain your energy also. Overeating puts a stress on the body and drains energy, as does eating in a hurried or agitated frame of mind. The most energy is obtained if the food is prepared mindfully and lovingly, is eaten in a harmonious and relaxed setting, with a sense of gratitude and awareness, and is well chewed until almost liquid so the saliva's enzymes can convert the carbohydrates to glucose for energy.

"The food itself is best if processed very little. Refined and fatty foods provide little sustenance and can actually drain energy, so it is best to avoid and limit the intake of products made with white rice, white sugar, white flour, hydrogenated or fractionated oils, chemicals, or preservatives. Organically grown whole grains and legumes, and fresh fruits and vegetables, as locally grown as possible, are best. Living foods, raw or moderately cooked, provide an abundance of enzymes, proteins, and easily available energy, and cleanse the body as they are utilized.

"As you well know, dead foods and foods of death, including all flesh foods such as beef, chicken, pork, fish, and shellfish, as well as foods containing any eggs, dairy products, or honey, pollute the body and mind with vibrations of killing, theft, manipulation, and abuse, and they inevitably reduce and distort energy. You certainly understand this, or you'd never have gotten this far. Carbonated beverages and chlorinated and fluoridated water ultimately sap energy as well, as do black tea, coffee, alcoholic beverages, tobacco products, and both commercial and non-commercial drugs, and would best be avoided, as far as possible.

"Besides healthy and vitalizing food habits, healthy elimination is essential for building energy. Following the above food guidelines will automatically provide ample fiber and also create clear, healthy blood and reduce any strain on the liver, kidneys, and bowels, and create a beneficial alkaline, as opposed to a toxic acidic, condition in the body-mind temple. Decaying fecal matter releases toxins and so regular elimination is essential, at least daily and preferably more often. An excellent idea is to train the body by going to the toilet upon arising every morning. If the elimination is slow in coming, gently massaging the abdomen in a clockwise direction may be helpful, as is assuming the natural posture of squatting instead of sitting. Putting your feet up on a footstool while sitting on the toilet is one way to do this. With practice, you will soon have regular morning eliminations, which is an energy-building way to begin the day.

"Another important factor in building energy is to live in beauty, generate beauty, and notice beauty, as closely to nature as possible. The chronic noise of machines tends to disturb and drain life energy, as does being in most modern buildings. There are many reasons for this enervation: the unnatural box motif that is relentlessly repeated; the electromagnetic fields produced by electricity and transmitters that permeate buildings and neighborhoods; the artificial and confining angles and shapes of living spaces, and the enormous heights these often are from the Earth; the toxic materials that are used, which contribute to high levels of indoor air pollution; the lifeless, chlorinated water in faucets, tubs, and pools, the deadened air caused by pollution, air conditioning, heating, and other ion-depleting factors; the grating noises and artificial smells that permeate these environments; the unnatural light and absence of unfiltered sunlight and of real darkness in these environments; and the staleness and lack of beauty which often characterize them.

"The silence and subtle sounds of nature and wildlife are food for your spirit and are a precious resource to be rediscovered, protected and enjoyed. Allowing your eyes and all your senses to experience the variety and beauty of nature is guaranteed to uplift your energy. Art and music that spring from deep reverence for life, from joy and love, and from communion with nature, are healing and energizing, radiating positive energy and beauty into man-made environments. Acoustic music, being born directly of the elements of the Earth, can typically generate more energy than electronic music. Living spaces that are alive, with gardens, organic shapes, plenty of light and fresh air and water, that are harmonious, serene, creative, and uplifting will tend to build the energy levels of those who are blessed by dwelling within them.

"Relationships can also build or drain your energy. A common mistake people make is to try to manipulate other people to get their energy. There are many different ways this is done, and they all result from non-meditative awareness. Without developing meditative inner silence, which requires a relatively high energy level and an intuitive understanding that you are not fundamentally separate from others, it is unlikely that you will be able to avoid the energy draining practice of manipulation. One common way people squander precious energy is in playing the role of victim, being the one who is chronically sick, or accident-prone, or confused, or just barely able to cope. By this manipulation of giving away their own energy, such people can unconsciously sponge attention and energy from others. Another energy-depleting role is being the one who is domineering, aggressive, dangerous, or abusive, and manipulating others through fear and in this way stealing their energy and attention. Another style is trying to please everyone and always make a good impression on others, thus manipulating them into giving energy. This is related to the habit pattern of forsaking one's own dreams and aspirations to please other people or to fit in. Another energy manipulating role is to be emotionally distant, so others must come begging, so to speak, hoping you're available. This is a way of sucking their energy and attention.

"The irony, of course, is that all of these unconscious ego strategies to accumulate energy by feeding on the energy of others lead, ultimately, to a drain on one's own energy, and can be draining on others as well, if they resonate at the same level. They can be addictive, creating vicious circles that spin through the cultural web of relations, as people unconsciously adopt different energy-manipulating strategies and compete for the limited amount of available attention, endlessly craving more recognition and approval, and never being actually satisfied. This frustration leads to conflict and further competition. Through meditation and building your own energy as we've been teaching, you can break free of these energy-draining patterns and unconscious addictions. The more you cultivate your connection with the your source, the less you'll be concerned with trying to get energy, attention, approval, and love from others. The manipulation game will automatically lose its appeal as its claws release you and you practice living in harmony with universal energy and allowing it to flow through your life more freely. As you do this, you'll be able to transmit energy to others as love, service, and support, and not be drained yourself, but in fact be invigorated by this.

"The main training to transcend these destructive relationship strategies, besides meditation and energy cultivation practices, is living an ethical life. The law of cause and effect is fundamental to all relationships. You are called to treat others as you would like to be treated, and this refers to humans, animals, ecosystem communities, and future generations. As your circle of caring grows, your energy field will expand. Thoughts, words, and deeds that are abusive of others, or manipulative of them, or that discount the inherent worth and dignity of others, will always lower your energy.

"There are five main precepts or guidelines of spiritual life that help with this, and they have inner and outer purposes. Their outer purpose is to bring more harmony and peace to relationships, and thus to the world. Their inner purpose is to help you act in ways that don't drain your energy and that support your spiritual path and your development of intuition. By cultivating these precepts assiduously, you can free yourself from addictive and frustrating relationships, become more conscious, heal your woundedness, and awaken your intuitive potential. Integrity and compassion are essential liberating forces in living an intuitive life, and the precepts encourage these forces. Eventually, as higher levels of consciousness and energy are maintained, the precepts are more effortlessly fulfilled because they are natural to spiritually mature people, but in the beginning they are mindfully practiced because the values of the culture you live in also live in you, and many of these cultural values violate the precepts in important ways. The five precepts are:

"1. 'Not to kill but to cherish all life.' This is the principle of *ahimsa* or harmlessness, and is the fundamental precept from which the others spring. It is to refrain from killing or injuring other people and sentient creatures by any action of the body, speech, or thought. It emphasizes cultivating an attitude of cherishing and protecting all expressions of life. As you go deeper into meditation, the wall between yourself and others will begin to dissolve and you will naturally become less narrowly self-interested. In the meantime, following this precept is a vital discipline that tames your mind and allows you to increase your energy level. Any attack on or neglect of another weakens you. Internalizing this precept creates a field of compassion and power around you, giving your words and actions weight with other people. It builds coherence between your highest aspirations and your actual daily life. The outer meaning of this precept involves, among other things, avoiding working for or investing in businesses that profit from harm to humans, animals, or ecosystems, avoiding animal-based food or clothing and animal-tested products because these cause animals to be killed and harmed, and in one's life refraining from attacking, criticizing, injuring or blaming others. The inner meaning is to cherish the seed of spiritual liberation that lies at the heart of all creatures, to see the highest potential in others, and to work for peace and freedom for all beings by cultivating the precious sprout of enlightenment within you. The deep inner meaning of this precept is to cherish and awaken to the present moment and its beauty and power, and not kill it by indulging in harmful or self-centered thoughts.

"2. 'Not to take what is not given, but to respect the things of others.' Flowing naturally from the first precept, the outer meaning here is to refrain from taking the property, life, time, or life-energy of others if it is not freely given directly to you. This precept emphasizes an attitude of respect for others, and especially encourages not discounting in your own mind the harmful effects that your negative actions, words, and thoughts have on others. The inner meaning is to avoid subtly attempting to steal the energy of others by manipulating them for attention or approval through all the methods discussed earlier. The deep inner meaning is to live in the fullness of each moment, and to give generously of your energy, attention, and resources in service to whatever raises your consciousness and, equally, the consciousness of your community.

"3. 'Not to engage in sexual misconduct, but to practice purity of mind and self-restraint.' Breaking this precept, or any precept, always brings suffering to oneself and to others. It is not that any of the actions prohibited by the precepts are evil in any cosmic sense; it is simply that they are unskillful. They invariably increase suffering, drain your energy, contract your spiritual field, and enmesh you

47

more deeply in the delusion of separateness and the greed, anger, fear, and grief that spring from this delusion. This precept again refers to any action of body, speech, or mind that sees another as an object for your own self-gratification. This is always degrading to others and to you. To use or abuse others sexually, because it is so intimate, is especially violating to them and energy-draining to you. On the inner level, this precept enjoins purity of mind, recognizing all beings as worthy of kindness and respect as expressions of life, endowed with inherent value. To devalue or harm others or use the vehicle of others or yourself for mere transitory pleasure is a violation of the dignity and sanctity of life. The deep inner meaning of this precept is to make an effort to understand the truth of interbeing that rejoices in the freedom of others, and gives openly without grasping or self-interest.

"4. 'Not to lie but to speak the truth.' This precept is potent and wide-ranging, and includes avoiding not just telling falsehoods or exaggerations, but any kind of deceitful action, word, or thought, as well as hypocrisy, fraud, and the gaining of unscrupulous advantage. Because the first precept is fundamental, telling the truth with intent to harm others is a violation and will drain your energy. The inner spirit of this precept is cultivating an attitude of straightforwardness and humility. It springs from and fosters fearlessness, and becomes more automatic as your practice of inner silence deepens and you mature beyond the manipulating stance that is so habitual in modern culture. The deep inner meaning of this precept is not to lie, internally or externally, by seeing others and yourself as mere material objects, but to speak the truth, awakening to the nature of all beings as related expressions of consciousness.

"5. 'Not to use or cause others to use liquors or drugs that confuse or weaken the mind, but to keep the mind clear.' This precept reminds you how important your own mind is. On the path of spiritual growth, your mind is your greatest ally, the precious vehicle through which you will transcend illusions and suffering and attain intuitive wisdom. Your mind has a vast potential, and can create both hells and heavens. Therefore it is essential to protect and purify your mind, and cultivate clarity and stability in your attention. Alcohol and drugs of all types tend to be harmful; they are outside agents that modify your body-mind and typically distract you from your path. Besides avoiding the more clearly damaging drugs such as alcohol, tobacco, cocaine, heroin, and mind-altering and 'mood-enhancing' pharmaceutical tranquilizers and stimulants, it is generally advisable also to avoid the more 'spiritual' and shamanic drugs like marijuana, peyote, psilocybin, LSD, and so forth.

"While you may think the experience of altered mental states and insights that these substances allow is helpful on your path, it seems doubtful they can confer spiritual maturity. If you have not developed the inner purity through meditation and right action that would allow these states and insights to develop within you organically, then they are ultimately of questionable value. These plants and chemicals allow you admittance to a show by sneaking you through the back door, but since you have not paid the entrance price through discipline and inner development, you may not be prepared to understand or properly embrace what you are shown. You may be frightened, or thrilled, or exalted, or receive revelations on the workings of the universe, but you may remain in some way deluded because of lacking the inner maturity to understand what you have experienced. This usually seems to be the case. Your ego will tend to add these experiences to its tale of being special, and your tail of tales may keep you stuck in the gate that you learned about on the Island of Understanding. Drugs typically do little to contribute authentically to intuitive living.

"The inner meaning of this fifth precept is that attempted shortcuts may lead to further trouble: addictions. The substance can be anything that removes you from the immediate experience of life, and for many in modern culture, television, social media, and main-stream media are destructive agents that insinuate themselves into your mind bringing disturbance and distraction. They are also prime outlets for the voice of corporate forces whose bottom line values are fundamentally contrary to all these precepts, and that work incessantly to chain you more deeply in delusion. Much of your culture's entertainment and spectator sports are also drugs of distraction that can drain your energy, and certain relationships are as well. Many of your compulsive habits may be distracting drugs if you look carefully. Perhaps by watching yourself closely you will discover helpful truths. Through this difficult work, your intuition is fed and will grow and flourish. The deep inner meaning of this precept is to refrain from indulging in the wine of delusion: to stop wandering the world in a culturally-indoctrinated trance, and make an effort to awaken to the wholeness that you are, the infinite beauty, light, and love that you are, and the freedom, joy, and compassion that you are!

"Investing your time and attention in endeavoring to embody these five precepts in daily life may help you purify your mind. Revelations, powers, and insights may begin to ripen within you in their right timing. We can only reap the fruits of the seeds that we actually sow. Nothing else can be harvested, and we can never outflank this universal principle. The precepts are guidelines that reflect this principle, and can help you cultivate the garden of your heart. This garden can bring forth beauty and nourishment, and from whatever seeds you cultivate, you reap your harvest.

"It seems that we harvest misery when we violate the spirit of these five precepts. Cultivating harmfulness or anger brings injury to others and conflict, pain, and hatred to us. Cultivating greed and jealousy leads to stealing from others, and lack, limitation, and discontentedness to us. Cultivating sexual craving and making objects of others brings fear, emptiness, and abuse to them and to us. Culti-

50

vating deceit and manipulativeness sows seeds of distrust and fear, and brings uneasiness, hatred, and pain to us. Cultivating a mind that looks for relief through escapes or unearned shortcuts causes further suffering to others and seems to bind us more tenaciously to our delusions. By cultivating the integrity, kindness, impeccability, sensitivity, and healthy self-restraint that the precepts indicate, we plant seeds of wisdom and inner peace. Perhaps the only shortcut to the Other Shore is in avoiding shortcuts.

"You see, the very ground that these precepts spring from is your true nature. There is within you an essential revulsion toward harming and manipulating others needlessly, and this is the essence of the first precept of non-injury. All the other precepts are extensions of it. As you continue in your efforts, you may more fully realize how willfully harming other humans or animals, or paying others to do so, inevitably disturbs and drains your energy, and hinders your evolution, as well as all your relationships with others.

"As you might assume, the energy we keep referring to is your spiritual energy. It may be possible to have an apparent abundance of physical, or intellectual, or emotional energy without having cultivated compassion and meditation, as you have for so long. But these energies may be misguided or misused, and will not endure, if there is a lack of corresponding spiritual energy. This spiritual energy can focus and raise these other types of energy enormously, even miraculously. In fact, without spiritual energy, these other kinds of energy are likely to be living on borrowed time.

"As you continue your efforts to build moral integrity, spiritual energy, and your capacity for awareness, you will find your relationships improving and becoming more rewarding. Through this cultivation, you may become more comfortable with being alone, if that frightens you, or being with others, if that frightens you. By cultivating spiritual energy, you will likely attract people who have similar values and commitments, and you will resonate together, effortlessly. By freeing others, you free yourself. Training with the precepts, you may become more honest and open with yourself, and also with others. Your intuition will automatically flower, as will peace and joy, through your dedication to non-injury and to developing spiritual energy. You may also be helping to build a more enlightened society as well.

"This brings us to another major key in your quest to build your spiritual energy, which is creativity. Many find that creativity and spirituality unfold together with intuition. All three may be doorways into healing. Cultivating any one seems to cultivate the other two, so that as you develop intuition, for example, you will likely find your creativity and spirituality are nourished. Fostering creativity may similarly nurture intuition and spirituality. When you are creative, you tend to be spontaneous and free from stale habits, fears, preconceptions, and judgments, and to allow your body-mind to be the vehicle for energy that is fresh and authentic. By practicing creativity, your potentials and spiritual energy may flourish like springs within you.

"There can be many creative avenues for your spirit to explore. There is musical creativity, expressing through rhythm, melody, and harmony, using instruments and voice, and using your body, through the timing and coordination of dance, movement, and many forms of athletics. The domain of artistic creativity is equally vast, working with color, space, line, form, and relationship, with rhythm and harmony through painting and sculpture, handcrafts and photography, and in the design of living spaces, clothing, jewelry, environments, meals, and countless inventions and innovations. There is also the whole arena of communication, teaching, writing, counseling, poetry, storytelling, drama, film, and community celebration. Life itself is an ongoing, endless splash of creative energy and are you anything other than an expression of that infinite creative loving force? It is in our cells to rejoice in creating.

"There seem to be two factors in creativity. One is practicing the craft and refining technical ability; the other is freeing the spirit within to unleash this craft and ability in higher and more fulfilling and inspiring ways. Whatever your creative medium at a given moment, improving your technical ability through hands-on engagement and practice can build your confidence and spiritual energy, and the power of expression. Even more energizing is the practice of creativeness itself. This is the practice of meditation in action and in daily life, living each moment freshly, letting go of chronically habituated patterns of thought and behavior, and living spontaneously, playing with ideas and experimenting with different approaches, toying with things, taking risks, trying out new ways of expressing yourself or relating with the world, and increasing the range of potentials you allow yourself.

"This seems to be encouraged by making an effort to be more flexible in your daily habits. You can mix things up and allow yourself to become more ambidextrous for example. Open doors, eat, carry things, and try writing more with your non-dominant hand. Play Ping-Pong, tennis, and other activities with alternating hands. You may find it helpful to take alternative routes to work and errands, and consciously notice the beauty around you, wherever you are. You can learn and practice other languages, travel to and explore other cultures, and try new activities, sports, crafts, and endeavors that give you a different perspective. Intuition seems to be fed by all this, and is nurtured by the ability to step out of ruts and habit-determined perspectives.

"As you walk down the street, can you look through the eyes of others and see the world they see, and can you discover your identity as a child, or elder, or homeless person, or person of another race, class, gender, ethnicity, or even a member of another species? How far can you stretch? Can you resonate with and walk in the world of the old woman, the young tough, the banker, the stray dog or cat, the wild blackbird? As you open to the fullness of all that you are, and question narrow social assumptions, your compassion and respect for others may grow, your understanding of them flourish, your energy field expand, and your intuition prosper. Practice is in the little efforts and leaps. Soon enough you may be able to make longer and bigger leaps. When you are ready, you may fly.

"As your energy builds, and your leaping ability increases, you may find your sense of humor improving. It will be easier to see a bigger picture, feel within yourself a larger heart, and discover humor, irony, joy, and meaning in places where they were previously undiscovered. Paradoxically, you may also find yourself open to greater pathos and to a more refined awareness of suffering and misery as your sensitivity and compassion grow. Your branches can reach as high as your roots go deep. This path of awakening may not be for the faint of heart! It seems that hypocrisy and self-centeredness may need to be sacrificed on the altar of compassion and adventure.

"There are more islands waiting as you journey toward the Other Shore, and they will expand on these themes in ways for which you are not yet prepared. As your energy increases, you will be able to understand and practice their message. For now, we leave you, but please remember: we are with you as you continue your journey.

"We leave you with this image for your muse to contemplate: a beautiful grand piano on a stage in a great hall filled with hundreds of eagerly expectant ears, and the musician, seated, launches into the music, but only plays one note. Over and over again, the same note, a B-flat, one note out of the eighty-eight on the keyboard. Alone, isolated, what little power this one note has, what little energy to evoke feeling, meaning, and inspiration! The audience's attention drifts and becomes perturbed as the musician plays only the same poor B-flat note over and over. People are looking at the exit doors when to their great relief another musician appears and displaces the first at the keyboard.

"This musician begins with the same ineffectual B-flat note, but moves on, up and down the keyboard, fingers flying as an enormous tide of music pours out of him through the piano and fills the room. The B-flat is now but one among many notes, and yet what power she has, what force! In certain passages, when her unique voice is heard among the others, there is such poignancy, then again, later, such pathos, and then again, such soaring joy! Her energy and power are now fully displayed, and they come from two things: she is true to herself and, too, she is part of something greater than herself and is true to that as well. Alone, she has little power, but together with the other notes, her potential is virtually limitless. As she sounds her B-flat voice truly and faithfully, and as the other notes do as well, the whole keyboard responds to the musician's touch, and every note contributes to the power and richness of every other note. Together they build a creation of beauty and feeling that is boundless in its potential.

"We appreciate your efforts to discover your own note, your unique voice, to contribute it, and to understand the source of all energy, the heart of the music, and the relationship of the notes. May your dance create a field of freedom that will bless everyone."

As we gaze now into the brilliant and loving eyes of this old gentleman shining before us, we feel energy tingling and rushing through our arms, legs, head, and torso, washing away old internal blockages and barriers. With a gentle and spacious gesture, he touches our forehead and the light around us becomes brighter. Pouring love toward us through his heart and smiling face, he slowly begins fading from us and gradually we find ourself sitting relaxed on the black sand beach on a warm, velvety night under a sky filled with stars. We hear music, and it begins with a plaintive B-flat note.

We listen as it ebbs and flows its haunting message to our heart. As it ends, we drift into a deep and restful slumber.

(For a trace of this music from the Island of Energy, please listen to piece number three, "Song of B-flat," on the accompanying album, *Islands of Light*.)

Chapter 3

The Island of Meditation

The morning dawns warm and bright, and we sit quietly with a feeling of thankfulness. After swimming in the cool waters of a nearby stream, we stretch and breathe, letting the energy within us expand and flow, practicing the techniques and attitudes we have learned here. The sense of beauty grows as we feel our energy rising, and the air shimmers around us. We spend several more weeks on this vibrant island, endeavoring to deepen our practice and contemplating the teachings we have received here. Eventually we feel the yearning to continue our journey. Saying goodbye to the Island of Energy and to our new friends, we feel their loving presence and thank them silently, smiling with the thought that though invisible, they may be watching us. And watching over us as well, we hope, succumbing somewhat to the relentless uncertainty of our ongoing voyage.

Sailing forth from the island, we lighten up, feeling suddenly invigorated and refreshed. Looking out over the waves swelling before us, we realize how *alive* the ocean is! Though this awareness includes an appreciation of the enormous variety of fish, birds, mammals, and other creatures teeming in and around the waters of the ocean, it goes beyond this to sensing the living presence of the ocean, and the pulsating waves of living energy that are coursing through it. Without thinking, we seem to be glimpsing the surpassing life of which the ocean is a spectacular manifestation. The immensity of this living presence overcomes us momentarily as we sense how far *beyond* the range of our conceptualizing this life is, how transcendent and magnificent.

We have a sense of realizing that we are like people who have been mistaking footprints in the sand for the one who *makes* the tracks. Obsessed with tracks and with following, categorizing, and analyzing them, we think we are experts in all types of footprints and tracks and that these footprints are real in and of themselves. Then one day we get a glimpse of the one who *makes* the tracks— why had we never thought to look for this one before? We sense that all living beings are like living footprints, manifestations of something far greater, something that is not a thing at all. What is that which makes all footprints, which casts all shadows? By looking somehow beyond and through and prior to the tracks we can perhaps intuit the presence that makes the tracks. The indescribable beckons. It is beyond and is *beyond* beyond.

We are brought down from our reverie eventually by pressing thoughts: which way is the next island? And where are we, anyway? Below us, the endless ocean of water, and above us, the endless ocean of space. We feel small and vulnerable. With an uncomfortable feeling of disorientation, we realize that we have no idea where we are or which way to head. The Other Shore seems impossibly distant, and we don't know in which direction the next island may be waiting.

Listening inside, we feel the familiar loving presence of the old gentleman of light from the Island of Energy. We feel a message emerge within us, that we are entering a higher level of vibration and that we can no longer rely on the sun and stars, or on our ship's compass and other instruments for guidance. Our guidance over the ocean must now come completely from within. We sense that somehow the ocean itself will be our guide. Though this seems nonsensical, we realize that we have no other alternative, as a glance at the sun's position and at the ship's compass reveals that it has stopped working. And so we make a leap of faith, and turn the ship's wheel while focusing on our connection with the ocean and with our heartfelt commitment to reach the Other Shore. Nothing. The ship swings slowly around. We continue rotating the wheel this way and that, listening intently within and praying for guidance. Still nothing.

We remember the teaching from the first island and let our prayer be a gentle and persistent receptivity to the sense we have of the eternal presence that is our source. We do our best to focus on this presence and let go of distractions and doubts. We open to understanding that this benevolent source is the origin of our intuition as well. We practice accepting and affirming this. We let go of thinking and simply feel thankful for our life and for this precious journey.

Drifting . . . Allowing . . . Not knowing . . . Trusting . . .

Suddenly we feel something within us gently click. Yes, this feels like the right direction. We feel an alignment as we continue in this new direction and if we stay alert and open to our connection with our purpose and our source, we find we can continue on with both confidence and a liberating sense of abandon. We know but we don't know how we know, and we know we better not think about it.

Out here on these pathless waters, our conventional mind has virtually nothing to cling to and in abandoning it, we see that the higher knowing of intuition is encouraged to emerge. It seems that our journey to the Other Shore, like life itself, is a koan. It is a quest and a question for which our conditioned rational mind alone can never provide effective guidance because its understanding is limited to the noisy operations of separating and comparing, whereas the intuitive heart understands by being silent, listening, and connecting. This higher understanding of intuition, though not trackable by rationality, is in fact trackable by intuition. This is how Zen masters taught and tested their students, how adepts communicated and, perhaps, how the science of the future will evolve to a more effective and holistic level.

As we continue on and let intuition guide us toward the Other Shore, we can sense that it is our openness to the larger patterns, and our sensitivity to them, that cues us at the ship's wheel. After several hours of sailing toward the empty horizon, we suddenly hear splashing and blowing sounds and see three dolphins swimming in front of us, and after a while, we sense that they are leading us. They occasionally disappear for a few minutes, but always return, cruising easily along and seem to be directing us across the waves. When evening comes, we can no longer see them and we stop sailing for the night, but the next morning, the dolphins are leaping off our bow, as if excited to start traveling again. We sail behind them for several days, wondering sometimes if they really know where the next Lost Island is, yet when we listen within, we always get a green light to continue to trust and follow them across the trackless expanse of waves.

Finally one morning, between the ocean of water below and space above, far out on the horizon off the port bow, we see an anomaly, a beguiling interruption, and our heart leaps with joy. Land! With heads nodding and somehow especially smiling, as if to say good-bye, the dolphins dive beneath the surface and we never see them again. With gratitude, we send them our heartfelt love for their guidance. The breeze is strong and we make good time, and by mid-afternoon we approach a mist-enshrouded island. Before long we're walking on the shore in the cool damp air. A deep sense of peace pervades this place. Instead of climbing through the forested hills above us and exploring the landscape, we feel it's right to just wait here quietly. A beautiful grove of tall palm trees seems to beckon to us and we walk over, sitting down comfortably on sand that is slightly green, shimmering in the late-day sun. We raise our energy and then direct our attention inwardly. After maybe twenty minutes, we hear a voice, warm and welcoming, as if greeting us from within.

"You have found the Island of Meditation. Well done! It is hard to get this far, but everyone does get here, sooner or later. While you're here you'll have the opportunity to learn more about the art of meditation. You are entering the heart of spiritual activity, and you'll discover that while it appears to be something you do and learn and train in, it is also not an activity in the usual sense, and isn't something you can master in the usual way. On this island, there are few limitations to the possibilities you can discover concerning the greatest of all mysteries, your own mind, and the greatest of resources, your true nature. You'll want to give all of your self and your energy to the practice here, and the fact that you've made it this far attests to the deep yearning of your heart. It is good that you trust this yearning and nourish it, and let it propel you forward on your quest.

"Without direct experience of the deeper and higher levels of consciousness attainable through meditation, can spiritual life be other than a secondhand affair? Isn't it similar to appreciating food through reading menus and recipes, rather than actually eating, tasting, swallowing, digesting, and incorporating the food and being vitalized by it directly? Since you've opened to the teachings of the first two islands, you may be ready to begin training in meditation. This is the training of attention. With practice, you may learn to bring your attention more fully into the present moment.

"When your energy and consciousness are strong and aligned, you may be able to enter *samadhi*, the absorption of your attention in one-pointed awareness and luminosity. In samadhi, you may realize directly the purity of your true nature, and that you are not your body, nor your perceptions, nor your feelings, nor your thoughts, nor even this self-conscious person that you have assumed yourself to be. You may step outside the prison of conditioned consciousness and see directly the vastness and joy that reflect the truth of your being. In samadhi, you can dwell beyond time and beyond the illusions that cause chronic contraction, fear, guilt, and suffering. You may realize your unity with what can be called the ocean of being that permeates everything. This is intuition in a pure form. Free from delusional separateness, the mind may be discovered to be inherently radiant.

"You perhaps understand that this awareness is available to those who persevere and make a sustained effort to purify their motives. The mind, after all, is slippery. The ego, a fabricated world centered on itself, suspects that meditative witnessing would reveal its insubstantiality. Its first line of defense, in a sense, in keeping its authority and existence unquestioned is a distracted mind that inattentively and anxiously wanders between past and future, fueling a continuous thought-stream that reinforces its sense of concrete separateness and rightness. It will slip, slide, and squirm with enormous vigor to avoid the silent clear awareness of samadhi. Drowsiness, frustration, excitation, boredom, relentless thinking, and self-importance are likely to be used.

"Have patience and perseverance. Your energy and motivation may be strongest when arising from the flame of yearning within your heart that remembers your connection with the infinite source. This can be seen as the call of your true nature. You are encouraged to focus steadfastly on this. You may have an unparalleled opportunity for your spiritual development here.

"Because of the sincere aspirations of generations of aspiring hearts, this island seems to be suffused with power. There is a field here that can allow you to progress in meditation more quickly than you would back on the shore you've left, with all the conflicted energies there. It is your efforts and aspirations that have brought you here to us. This is the way it always is. When an inner doorway opens, be it for good or ill, then outer doorways may open to serve the inner. This island is such a doorway, and it seems best to maintain your focus on the truths you've been learning. It's not a good idea to indulge in blame, fear, discouragement, or anger. You're entering domains of higher power through your practice of meditation, and any negativity you yield to may have more serious consequences.

"The most beneficial teachings tend to come from within, when the mind clarifies and abides in witnessing awareness. To help you experience these teachings and awaken your intuitive wisdom, you may like to enter a meditation retreat, beginning tomorrow morning if that is amenable. You will find a meditation hut down on the beach, not too far away, comfortable and quiet, and we'll be ready to begin at four o'clock a.m. You can meditate as much as you like."

The next morning comes, and the teachings begin. Rising, we notice how energized we feel, despite the early hour. After some energy-raising exercises, we sit, awaiting instructions.

Again, the voice comes to us:

"The first meditation practice we'd like to teach you is called the Four Viharas. It's an ancient practice that countless people have found to be helpful in purifying the mind and heart, and creating a more solid foundation for the meditations that will follow. This practice, though, is certainly not limited just to beginners. *Vihara* is a Sanskrit word meaning abode or home, and the purpose of this practice is to return to your inner home, which has four aspects: *maitri*, or love; *karuna*, or compassion; *mudita*, or joy; and *upehka*, or peace. By cultivating love, compassion, joy, and peace, you'll be purifying and beautifying your inner environment. It's this inner environment that seems to be crucial because you bring it everywhere. By cleansing and uplifting this inner feeling environment, you'll be doing some of the essential work to help bring love, compassion, joy, and peace into our outer world as well. With this Four Viharas practice of acknowledging and returning to your true home, you have your hands on a vital key to intuitive living. Cultivating these four unlimited inner states can heal old wounds that keep your mind distracted and anxious.

"One of the universal principles seems to be that the outer flows from the inner. The outer can also affect the inner, but you seem to be on the path of discovering the primacy of the inner, and the power you carry within you. When used in conjunction with the five precepts you learned about on the Island of Energy, the Four Viharas practice can plant seeds of healing within and bring joy and peace into your world.

"The old question of how to work with negative emotions has been wisely answered with the idea that rather than either repressing them or acting them out, you can learn to bring the light of awareness to these emotions, watching and inquiring. The practice of the Four Viharas, though, goes even further than this by actually transforming the energy that would otherwise manifest as a contraction of anger, jealousy, greed, fear, or irritation. It opens the mind and raises energy so that, for example, instead of feeling personally attacked in a particular situation, you begin naturally and genuinely to feel compassion and kindness for others who are perhaps acting in aggressive or thoughtless ways because of their wounding and suffering.

"Compassion, like intuition, is strengthened as you use it, like a muscle. Practicing the Four Viharas and strengthening your connection with your inner home, you become more willing and able to listen deeply to others and to understand them. Through the Four Viharas, you have the opportunity to harmonize your inner and outer worlds through inner cleansing and cultivation. You needn't repress, or act out, or even alertly watch whatever negativity arises within yourself because it naturally transforms into lovingkindness by the presence in your consciousness of the Four Viharas. Through patient and regular practice, your mind becomes established in this space, its home.

"Although you may think you are practicing the Four Viharas, the 'you' that is practicing is actually the obstacle to the free functioning of the Four Viharas, which represents the abode of consciousness when it is released from the delusion that it is a separate thing. When this release happens, the lovingkindness, compassion, joy, and harmony of your true nature seem to return and fill the field of awareness with their light, which may actually be your light. The Four Viharas are vast, and represent the liberated mind's response to the arisings of the world when it is intuitively open and free of the ego's tale. The Four Viharas are often called the Four Immeasurables.

"This is the actual practice: begin by becoming aware of your breathing. With every exhalation, letting go of thinking, and entering more deeply into the present moment. Let go of any thoughts pertaining to the past or future. Open to the awareness that you are now giving yourself a beautiful gift: you are giving your highest

65

aspiration your undivided attention. Do your best to clearly realize that for the time of practicing this meditation, you won't need to think at all of outside concerns, plans, or problems. To engage in meditation is to step out of the stream of thinking and out of the world of your self-concern. So, to continue:

"With each exhalation letting go of thinking, and with each inhalation engendering within your heart the feeling of love. Allow this feeling of love to wash into your heart, filling it with every inhalation. With every exhalation, letting this feeling of lovingkindness flow out into the world, filling the space around you with love. This love is a feeling of benevolence and goodwill, of yearning that all others are happy and blessed with the causes of highest happiness. Breathe in this love, and then exhale, radiating lovingkindness. Experiencing this quality of pure love, how it feels in your heart, in your body, and in your mind, beyond thinking. If distracted, relaxing and returning to love, engendering and radiating love. Feeling this love as being universal like the warmth of the sun: with every exhalation, shining love to those who are close to you, to those who are neutral, and even to those who are distant or difficult for you. Radiating love to all, breathe and allow lovingkindness to flow to every being in your world. Send love to yourself as well, loving the unique and precious being that you are, with appreciation and warmth. Allowing that feeling of love to expand, you become a breathing, living fountain of love, shining love in all directions to all beings, like an ever-expanding sphere, breathing and radiating love...

"Now with every inhalation, engendering in your heart the feeling of compassion. This is a feeling of caring, of wishing others to be free from suffering and from all causes of suffering, and of yearning to actively relieve their suffering. With every exhalation, allowing this feeling of compassion to radiate from your heart, filling the space around you with the energy of compassion. Inhaling compassion, allowing it to fill your heart and every cell of your be-

66

ing, and exhaling, letting compassion flow forth to all beings who are in any way suffering, and filling the world around you with empathy and compassion. Breathing compassion, becoming compassion, and being the living embodiment of compassion: allowing this feeling to radiate like an ever-expanding sphere around you, shining the light of compassion, including all beings in the field of compassion, and filling the world with compassion...

"With every inhalation, engendering the feeling of sympathetic joy in your heart. This is a feeling of opening to and delighting in the joys of others and in the world around you. It is the pure joy of being: joy in the cycles of life, in the endless vistas of becoming, and in the adventure of living. This is the great joy that needs no reasons or outer causes. Allow this joy to come bubbling into your heart and into every cell of your being. With every inhalation, this transcendent joy is filling your heart, and with every exhalation, the truth of this joy is overflowing from your heart, filling every cell in your being and pouring out through your skin, filling the space around you with joy, and filling the entire world with the truth of joy. Breathing and radiating the boundless joy of being, allowing it to radiate out from you like an ever-expanding sphere, filling the world with the light and energy of vibrant, transcendent joy...

"With each inhalation, engendering in your heart the feeling of peace. This feeling of peace arises effortlessly from your understanding that you are always and irrevocably connected with the radiant web of living consciousness, and with the loving source of all life. For the heart filled with love, compassion, and joy, peace arrives naturally. The feeling of peace flows into your heart, mind, and body with every inhalation, and you open to this feeling of harmony and serenity. With every exhalation, allowing the energy of peace to flow out from your heart, and feeling your heart as the heart of the universe. Breathing and radiating peace and harmony, allow this feeling to permeate every cell of your being and radiate

67

outward, filling the world and the universe with the truth of all-embracing peace....

"Breathing love... compassion... joy... and peace....

"Radiating love... compassion... joy... and peace....

"Abiding in love... compassion... joy... and peace....

"Being love... compassion... joy... and peace....

"Love ... Compassion... Joy... Peace....

"Continue with the Four Viharas meditation, breathing and radiating love... compassion... joy... peace....

"Love... compassion... joy... peace....

"Coming home to your true home, abiding in love... compassion... joy... peace... love... compassion... joy... peace...."

As the voice fades, we continue meditating on these four limitless states. We open to feeling the essence to which each word is pointing. A sense of inner stretching, of enlarging our heart, and sometimes of pulling down inner walls accompanies the practice as the hours go by. We feel an energy field developing around us as we continue radiating the Four Viharas in ever-expanding spheres around us from our heart. Eventually we feel that what we are *is* love, compassion, joy, and peace. The words themselves fade away at one point as we breathe and dwell in a state that is deeply relaxed and flowing, and also highly energized and alert. Around mid-morning we gather and eat some fruits, and we continue practicing, absorbed in the Four Viharas.

The kind voice returns to us: "The Four Viharas practice has begun its work in you, purifying and revealing. During this retreat you have no obligations other than fully entering the spirit of meditation and self-discovery. You can take two meals daily, provided by the abundant fruits here, and can feel free to walk the beach or hills for refreshment. The focus, of course, is the meditation, and it is best to continue practicing while eating, walking, and even while sleeping. It's very possible here.

"If you devote yourself fully for one week to this Four Viharas practice, you may be ready for the next practice. As you know, while sitting, be sure to keep your posture erect so the energy can flow properly and so you'll stay alert, and it's best to refrain from moving, except when you rise to stretch, walk, or eat. The discipline of taming the fidgeting body-mind can help you return to your true nature. If you should have any questions or need assistance, just ask. We're here for you."

During the afternoon meal, we practice the Four Viharas, and return, again and again, over the next week, to the sanctuary of sitting in silence, engendering and radiating the Four Viharas. Many side effects arise and, as we are instructed, we continue practicing. Sometimes we see beautiful lights, white and intense, or colored. We feel aching pressures in different places, at first in our legs and body and, later in the week, in the region of our heart. While walking we are sometimes dazzled by the brightness and presence of a tree, flower, bird, or rock, and as we look, find their beauty to be heart touching. Seeing without the old habitual inner commentary, the world becomes increasingly magnificent, and almost overwhelming in its intricacy and poignancy. At times we feel faint and have to rest.

Difficulties arise also, old fears, hurtful memories, regrets and guilt. At first they are disturbing until we are able to simply offer them like firewood to the Four Viharas fire glowing within us. Tears and even sobbing erupt at one point. Energy pours through us, cleansing and washing away old debris. At times it is excruciating. We have somehow entered the spirit beyond the four words, and it is taking us apart, wound-by-wound, knot-by-knot, and thought-by-thought. In the pervasive brightness of the Four Viharas, there is no room for fear, regret, pride, or the old tale of self. We discover layer upon layer of mental states and repressed feelings, revealed through the power of this practice, in spite of the ongoing distractions from our habituated ways of thinking.

Love, compassion, joy, and peace: it becomes all we know and all we need to know. There seems to be a current of power on this island that pulls us along, allowing us to enter more deeply into silence. This current invites us to take inner risks, dissolving old chunks of fear and distrust, and massaging away cramped mental tightness. We find our mind softening and becoming a flowing stream. At times it seems we have never worked so agonizingly hard; at other times it all seems utterly effortless as we float along watching everything. By the end of the week, we are deeply quiet, observing, and as if finally unshackled inside, free to observe and enjoy the arisings of the day. Love, compassion, joy, and peace are well worn, trusted friends, and like any trusted friend, worthy of only our best effort. They have become the eyes and ears of a new being that seems to be emerging within us. We hear the voice of our teacher within us again:

"Yes! Perhaps you are giving birth, and returning home, ascending to your place in the magnificence of creation, relieved of many painful illusions. The process is unfolding, like the blossoming of a flower. It is completely natural. Your practice now can shift to mindful awareness, watching and listening attentively. This can be seen to be the heart of meditation practices, and is perhaps the essence of prayer.

"As you may already know, the Four Viharas is but one among a myriad variety of meditation practices. These practices all provide an object for the mind to dwell on or contemplate. Visual practices are examples of this, and there are innumerable visualization practices from many traditions. Some are relatively simple, visualizing a candle flame, or a letter, or the sky, or a *yantra*, or a geometric shape, and some, like the mandalas, are exceedingly complex, like the refuge tree of the Tibetan Buddhists, containing hundreds of images.

Some practices are more auditory. There are simple recitations, or tones, like prayers, mantras, and chants. There are long and complex prayers, mantras, and chants as well, and meditations upon different types of sound. These visual and auditory practices are universal and effective, and they also include meditations on words, like the divine names, the Four Viharas, and other practices. Besides these, there are also many meditation practices that focus more on physical sensations and movements. These may be found within the traditions of yoga, of pranayama, of Qi Gong and Tai Chi, of whirling and dance of countless types, and even of certain athletic practices.

"One of the most universal meditation practices, attentiveness to the breathing, is also of this type. Breathing is perhaps the main ongoing physiological process that is easily either conscious or unconscious. For the untrained mind, breathing is mainly unconscious and shallow, and this directly contributes to the proliferation of wandering thoughts and conflicted emotions that ordinary human consciousness routinely experiences. However, by becoming conscious of the breathing, the mind can return to the present moment and become more peaceful, receptive, and aware.

"As you have perhaps discovered, bringing consciousness to the process of breathing may initiate a naturally meditative state that is energizing and harmonizes your emotions. It may be especially helpful to pay attention to your breathing in stressful or irritating situations. According to research, when breathing is unconscious, it is typically controlled by the more primitive parts of the brain, which are also the seat of the fight-flight survival response, and of fear and anger. By attending to your breathing, your consciousness naturally moves to higher levels within you that observe situations peacefully rather than reacting to them.

"Breath meditation is in a very real sense the mother of all meditations, and by making your breathing conscious, slow, and deep, your mind may become more balanced and open to intuition.

Whales and dolphins, like your friends who guided you to this island, are mammals like you who breathe consciously throughout the day, even while sleeping. Their continuous practice of mindful breathing is one reason they have developed a consciousness that may be in some ways more refined than human consciousness. Like them, you can meditate by bringing attention to your breathing and benefit by it significantly.

"The number of meditation practices that people have evolved to help focus, deepen, and awaken consciousness, and the variety of these practices, would fill volumes. There are extensive systems in the various Buddhist, Taoist, Hindu, and Jain traditions, the Jewish, Christian, and Islamic traditions, the shamanic traditions, and in the ancient Greek, Persian, Egyptian, and Mayan traditions, and many more besides these, and more are being rediscovered and created all the time. This rich heritage of meditation techniques is one of humanity's great treasures, and its enormous breadth seems to be more available to people in your time than ever in history. Meditation practices have the same object: to bring the mind into a state of peace, a focused awareness and watchfulness abiding in the present moment. Through this, the original brightness of the mind returns, and this brightness, shining unimpededly, fosters intuitive understanding and lovingkindness.

"It could be said that these are all meditations with form. There is always an object, subtle or less subtle, of one's attention or devotion. Through these practices, the mind is healed; it connects into the immediacy of the present moment and into its basic wholeness. Distracting thoughts recede and the mind concentrates on the object of one's practice. The mind must first be tamed; then it can be trained to penetrate the veils of illusion.

"Form meditations can eventually lead to formless meditation, and this can be seen as the hidden heart of meditation. With formless meditation there is no longer an object of devotion or concentration. Spiritual maturity can help bring you to this point. As you've learned, abiding by the precepts of ethical conduct is essential. By eschewing cultural habits of negligence and self-preoccupation, you can begin participating in the liberating adventure of discovery at the cosmic level that is available to the tamed and trained mind.

"The spirit of the Four Viharas seems to be alive in you, and you recognize the folly of seeking gain or pleasure at the expense of others, or through pursuits in the outer world. Your regular daily meditation practice that prepared you for this journey to the Other Shore has served you well. Now it seems to be time for the next step; we will instruct you in formless meditation.

"Formless meditation is silent inner awareness. If your energy is strong and pure, you will be able to enter inner silence with little effort. Otherwise you are called to understand that there is nothing in the world of form or in the world of thought that can fulfill your heart's longing. When you come to the point where you understand this thoroughly, you will be able to let go. Letting go of thinking, of grasping, of becoming, of being: this is a key to meditation and to awakening. As you understand the nature of the world of sense objects and thoughts, and their ephemerality, you tend to free yourself from craving and aversion, and your mind can return to its natural state. This is samadhi, one-pointed luminous awareness. In meditations with form, samadhi is experienced as communion, blissful and profound. In formless meditation, samadhi is completely non-dual, and while difficult to describe or discuss, can be remarkably liberating.

"Although the energy field of this island may help you, you are called nevertheless to exert yourself to understand, experience, and embody this. Your practice now is to enter the silence of witnessing awareness, beyond movement of the mind. You are ready. All your lifetimes have brought you to this point, as have your years of seeking. Your efforts in retreats and in daily meditation, and your endeavors to cultivate kindness for others through mindfulness and simple living, and to question, awaken, and serve, have helped create the necessary foundation. No exertion has been lost. Each has helped bring you here, poised on the brink of new dimensions.

"Let nothing distract you now! We invite you to begin by remembering your motivation to awaken for the benefit of all life. You work not just for your own inner realization, but also, as you know, for all beings, your brothers and sisters, to better serve the life that is all of us.

"You can begin by allowing your attention to rest on your breathing, and through this, become aware of your connectedness with all beings. Let go of thinking, and simply be aware of your breathing. If a thought arises, let it go the instant you are aware that you are thinking, and return to awareness of your breathing."

We continue with this meditation on mindful breathing for fifteen or twenty minutes until we hear our inner teacher speaking.

"Continue breathing, and now let go of attending to your breath and just listen. Intently, listen within. No thought arises because your attention is devoted completely to listening. Open and receptive, you dwell in inner silence, listening. There does not need to be a listener for listening to be present. You understand that thinking avails nothing, so you can abandon it completely. If your mind wanders, you can support this inner listening with simple breath awareness. Aware of each breath and listening. Witnessing whatever arises and returning to the practice of listening. Always return to the inner listening."

Hours pass, and days pass. In outer silence, all our time is passed in sitting or walking meditation, and eating a little food. At first things go smoothly, but after a few days our mind rebels, and seems to want nothing more than to chatter incessantly. Like a mother cat patiently bringing her ever wandering little kittens back,

74

we return, over and over, to the still point of awareness as inner listening. The hours are often difficult as our mind jumps around or else gets foggy, dreamy, and dull. We rouse ourself to vigilance and bring attention as fully as we can to the practice of alert receptivity.

Eventually, we reach a certain point at which everything gradually changes. Our mind begins to relax and focus. As it becomes more absorbed in the practice, we seem at times to disappear and then the listening itself seems to be doing the practice. At these times we find that we no longer need to try to do the practice. Our mind seems to dwell fully and spontaneously in the quiet openness of simply listening within. Our breathing becomes subtle and at times seems to almost completely disappear. A peculiar sensation gradually grows within us of an unstoppable energy arising and propelling its way through every movement and moment.

As we continue through the hours of practice, sitting quietly, just listening, we find that our unwavering and open attention gradually builds and becomes a potent wave. Rolling along, its power increases. It gathers momentum. It becomes an unstoppable, irresistible force. It transcends us and moves us and we know the answer to the old question: the immovable object moves. It seems that nothing can resist this wave that is carrying us on and on. Its power becomes enormous, overwhelming.

Fully present, we let go over and over again. The present moment is all there is. We surrender more completely, and expand beyond thinking and beyond being anyone or anything. Just listening. Our mind is intensely focused in the present, and yet open, beyond boundaries, words, and concepts. We reach a sense of timeless eternity, a sense of being beyond striving or attaining.

Something lets go within. Light engulfs everything, and we disappear. Everything disappears, and there is effortless release, deep silence and peace. No words or thoughts, and no one to be, to prove, to live or die. Radiant presence with no separation and nothing ever to be separate. Inexpressible vastness. Silence shines and releases and spins. Fluidity. Dwelling beyond words in timelessness....

Moments are eons are moments....

Eventually we begin returning, filled with luminous joy. Words and beings are drops and sparkles in the ocean of consciousness. What we are is eternal and Real. We have never been anything but the light that lights up every being! Unborn and undying light. The little self, like a painted light bulb—how quaint and cute, with all its posturing, we view it with enjoyment and appreciation. All the little selves: a profusion of sculpted and painted light bulbs. We see it clearly. Fleshly bodies come and go, illumined by the Real, shadows of the Real, hiding places for the Real. Only the Real is real! In bursting joy, we are the whole blooming, endless and beginningless dance, and the divine matrix, and assuredness, and timelessness....

We return to the harbor of our mind as if returning from the great ocean, and there seems to be mainly gratitude, and a sense of fluid freedom. We meditate in silence for several days, whole and bright, basking in life. We begin to walk around the island a little. The windows of all our senses have been washed clean, and heart-wrenching beauty surrounds us.

The sight of a little frog sends tears running down our cheeks. The sky and sun, flowers, pebbles, ants, and trees. Everything reveals the Real! It is all unspeakably delightful! How could we have possibly been so blind for so long? We look and listen, our mind unmoving and present. How lush it all is. We rake the little yard outside our hut and have never been more thrilled by any activity. Words fail to convey the feeling of freedom and poignancy, as if the infinite love shining at the heart of the universe is doing its job, raking leaves and pebbles. All the old koans and conundrums dissolve. The field! The gate! The little tail! The ox. How obvious and plain and precious it all is.

Slowly, over the next week, our illuminating experience becomes a memory. Words, thinking, and personal experience all begin reasserting themselves. We still dwell in a deep and radiant peacefulness, but the disturbance of self-preoccupied thinking, and of our concern about the suffering in the world we left behind us, slowly insinuates itself back into our experience. Our inner teacher returns.

"Yes, there may be no words to express the peace, freedom, and awareness potentially available in this eternal moment. This is clear to you now. Words and thinking always occur within a relatively small harbor of the mind. In fact, the shared cultural world of thinking, speaking, expressing, and experiencing, no matter how shallow or profound, simple or complex, no matter how uplifting or depressing, still occurs within the harbor of the shared cultural mind. Leaving this harbor, leaving words and thoughts behind, the mind enters the ocean of consciousness. This ocean is boundless, with countless shores, and is teeming with light. It fills a multitude of harbors and gives rise to untold potentials of being and of experience.

"Entering this ocean, you enter your true nature, and leaving words behind, you leave the conditioned self behind, and leave personal experience behind as well. Spiritual awakening seems to be impersonal. As you now understand, you, personally, could never experience the ocean of being. Your self-preoccupation was dissolved by the unstoppable momentum of continuously open and undistracted attention. It was only then that 'you' could enter the ocean of being, though the self that entered was certainly not the personal self you ordinarily take yourself to be. That was left behind, like shoes at the door of the temple.

"Entering this ocean, you are the ox entering the field. Your tail hangs small and humbly behind you. Describing anything confines it, actually. As soon as we think or speak, words bring us into and keep us within the harbor, while all around us, the luminous open ocean surges and shines.

"Now your practice will actually begin. You have glimpsed the Other Shore. You have tasted your original nature and seen directly what can never be taught by another or described in words. It is a gift that you could never earn, and yet you have attained it. No effort is ever lost in this great journey of awakening. You will perhaps never be the same smaller self again. You've seen directly, and the light within you is brighter now. Your practice will be different because you have this foundation.

"Before this, your practice was more like groping in the dark, trying to follow and interpret teachings, trying to trust, and more groping. Now the lightning has flashed and you have seen the landscape. You have left the harbor and glimpsed the ocean. From now on your practice will be to bring your entire life—every thought, word, and deed—into harmony with what you've experienced. Your challenge now is to embody and live what has been revealed to you.

"A helpful way to do this is through practicing mindfulness, meditation, and prayer, and the essence of all three is the pure awareness of samadhi. We speak of *absolute samadhi* as the inner meditative state of profound stillness that occurs while sitting quietly, as you experienced here. This is the foundation of *positive samadhi*, which is the practice of living in a meditative state, whatever activities you are engaged in. Positive samadhi is mindfulness, being fully present in the activities of daily life such as cleaning, walking, and creating. It is breathing with awareness, with attention devoted to each action, fully in the now. You are likely to feel less attached to the results of your actions because you're less bound by a sense of separateness. It has been called doing without doing, and it is possible, as the witness rather than the doer of the actions, to access higher levels of energy, clarity, and skillfulness in the words and deeds performed through you, than if your words and deeds spring from your conditioned thinking and motivation.

"As you let go of the sense of being personally invested in your actions, and let go of conditioned assumptions about who you are and how life is, you'll be more centered in the present. Because your motives will no longer revolve around furthering the interests of your separate self, you'll be a giver and a healer without thinking of giving and healing. By your awareness that you are far more than the little object self you learned about on the first island as the ox's tail, and by your deep listening, you may naturally help to bring more peace and freedom to the world. Your understanding may radiate from every gesture and inform your underlying attitude. As you practice the mindfulness of positive samadhi in your daily activities, it will naturally be easier to enter the inner silence of absolute samadhi. This will further support not only your practice of mindful and intuitive living, but also your understanding of prayer.

"Prayer, like meditation, is natural and healthy. The old Aramaic word means to be open like a trap, utterly open and receptive. This may be thought of as *absolute prayer*, which is similar to the inner expectant silence of absolute samadhi in the meditation tradition. Absolute prayer is being open to the ocean of which you are a wave, and there may be an element of profound yearning as well. *Positive prayer* is also known as *affirmative prayer,* and is the understanding that emerges spontaneously from the realization of absolute prayer. It is the understanding that the wave is fundamentally the ocean itself, a unique face arising from and one with the ocean.

"Positive prayer is intuitively understanding that there is ultimately no power in opposition to the benevolent all-embracing force that is your source, and is the source of all manifestations. Understanding that this source alone is real, whatever the outer appearances may be, brings healing. This ground of being is in all being, and all being arises in this infinite being. Though prayer may

79

contain yearning, it can culminate in this higher understanding, which we term positive prayer. There is also the kind of prayer that asks for something and is based on an underlying assumption of separateness. This dualistic prayer can eventually become an impediment to your awakening if it reinforces the overt or subtle sense of separateness and the clinging and fear that are unavoidably associated with this sense of separateness.

"Meditation and prayer are both experienced as inner silence in their absolute aspects. In their positive aspects, they bring this experience into the situations of daily life. Meditation becomes mindful awareness, and prayer becomes understanding the allness of the infinite source, and respecting others and yourself as living expressions of this source.

"It is essential to avoid the attitude that you are somehow special and superior to others because you've had a glimpse of these truths. This is a poison to your unfoldment, and can easily lead to inflation and to suffering. There is some truth to the old saying that the higher one goes, the farther will be the fall.

"We invite you to be vigilant! Life is ever flowing, always flowering into fresh possibilities, and perhaps the greatest contribution you can make is your example and your effort to embody your unfolding understanding. You seem to be established on the path, and your practice of living the truth you have discovered here can continue and bear fruit. Let every act be consecrated to the unfolding of wakefulness in your daily life.

"This retreat is coming to an end soon. Your motivation is on firmer ground. You have tasted freedom. Your practice now is to embody the precepts and this understanding. Your intuition can flower as your mind leaves the confines of the harbor in which it has been abiding and moves out into the ocean, to freely roam and touch on every land and to every depth. Then you may find yourself on the Other Shore.

"In the Zen tradition, a way of practice and of cultivating and testing one's intuitive wisdom is to contemplate a koan, which is, as you know, a profound question that can only be solved by the direct seeing of intuition. As you realize from your experience on the Island of Understanding, the rational mind can never penetrate a koan. By meditating on the koan's riddle in the proper way, though, the koan may eventually be a success, breaking the hold of dualistic conditioned thinking and revealing in a flash the profound truth of being. The most ancient of all koans is the question we all face: 'Who am I?' or "What am I?' or as it is sometimes phrased, 'What is my original face before my parents were born?'

"Another koan, one of the most well known, is this: 'What is the sound of one hand clapping?' You know the sound of two hands clapping, but what is the sound of one hand? Everything is symbolic. The sound of two hands clapping is this world of form: everything you can see, hear, taste, touch, smell, and think about. This koan of one hand clapping is designed to turn the mind in a completely different direction, toward the pure potential out of which this world of form emerges, and to which it returns again, moment by moment. Every sound emerges out of silence and eventually returns to silence again. Every form arises from infinite space and eventually returns to space again. Every being can be seen, perhaps, as a melody, a unique song that emerges from silence, is heard for a while, carried on the wind, and that eventually returns to silence again, like a wave emerges from and returns to the ocean.

"What is this silence, this source, this ocean, this sound of one hand clapping? To help find out, you can enter the space between thoughts, the silence between the notes of music. Then you may know directly, which is the way of authentic understanding. You can listen for the silence while you sit in silence, and this is an excellent practice, and another helpful practice is to listen for the silence while listening to appropriate music. Listen to the spaces between the notes as well as to the notes, and to the patterns of silence within the patterns of sound. Become sensitive to silence, comfortable with it, and learn to dwell beyond thinking in the pure act of listening. You can understand the sound of one hand clapping. And this understanding can help bring wisdom and freedom. We have some music for you to try this with; please listen for the sound of one hand, the silence within the music, the space between the notes. Listen deeply. What do you notice?"

(For a trace of the music that comes wafting through to us while we open to this practice on the Island of Meditation, and to try it yourself, please listen to piece number four, "Song of Inner Spaces," on the accompanying album, *Islands of Light*.)

For the last few days of our island meditation retreat, we sit in silence, allowing all the teachings and insights we have received to sink in more deeply, and we take some long walks along the beautiful beaches. At times, quietly sitting, aware of the breathing, or deep in relaxed and silent walking, the haunting music of the one-hand meditation washes through us, and we realize how vibrant and alive silence is, so immediate, containing all potentials. We can scarcely contain the uprushing power that seeks, it seems, to flood us in its vastness. We are slowly coming to understand the liberating effect that watchful, open, and receptive awareness brings, connecting us with the ever-present silence that makes every sound possible.

On this island, we feel we have been completely worked over, softened like clay in the fingers of a strong and loving hand. A crust around our heart has been broken and pulled away, and we walk by the ocean, feeling our heart's soft flesh, sensitive, vulnerable, open, and pulsing. Something has died, and a new birth seems to be underway. It will soon be time to sail on, continuing our journey to the Other Shore. We breathe love, compassion, joy, and peace. We wander a little more in the exquisite beauty here, wrapped in the unfamiliar sense of freedom that arises as we watch our thoughts and actions from a new space of bright and detached awareness.

Chapter 4

The Island of Imagination

Sailing on, we skim over azure waters that stretch in seeming eternity in every direction under the warm subtropical sun. After the Island of Meditation, we feel profoundly peaceful, and with a sense of serene confidence we plunge further into the unknown. Everything seems different to us now; perhaps the old sailors were right after all, and we have indeed sailed over the edge of the world.

We have perhaps, at least, sailed over the edge of ourself. The sense of peace is still surprising. We have gone beyond our usual self-identification; we are this journey, and the Other Shore, and the ocean, and the sky, and the ship that seems to be traveling. We are the goal and the path and the great force that holds it all. More free now of concepts and concerns, we listen within and let the sky direct our hand on the ship's wheel. We feel the next island beckoning to us across the miles and across the days, and we open to guidance from the clouds and from the great blue dome that arcs over us. When we go too far to port or starboard, we feel it, and move back again, sailing on, responding to promptings from the sky and from the horizon. Gratitude shines in our heart.

Feedback, the foundation of intelligence, guides us. Opening our awareness, we respond and adjust. We see that this is how our intuition develops, and how we know if it is "right." Good old feedback! We feel as if we have climbed up to the sill of the window between the two worlds, and can see both sides of the feedback dance, and how they prompt each other. On one side, we can see our self, open and responding to our not-self (which is the world that seems outside and other), and on the other side, we can see our not-self, open and responding to our self. Back and forth go the feedback interchanges, like tennis volleys through the window, and we see that self and not-self are enraptured with each other, delighting in the play. Both self and other are vast and unknown, and we glimpse their unity in a moment of clearly seeing that there can never be any mistakes. Infinite life manifests as self and not-self; we smile and the sky smiles back; the sky smiles, and we smile back.

Feedback! Intelligence is exquisite, streaming through the play of self and other, brightening as the wall between them dissolves. Separateness falling away, we see it: as the knower disappears, feedback transcends itself, becoming simultaneous, instantaneous, and continuous. Feedback happens within itself! Even with all the appearances to the contrary, feedback always happens within itself. We are not separate from the world. This is how intuition knows, as feedback arising within itself.

This understanding washes through us as we look out over the waves toward the horizon. Above us, we suddenly hear the sound of flapping wings. A large white albatross has landed on the top of our mast. He takes off, flying ahead of us, and we feel warmth in our heart for this feathered being whose strong wings carry him securely between sky and sea.

We feel guided to sail behind the albatross, though he often flies beyond our view, and then sits resting on the water, waiting for us, or else circles around and flies over our ship as if to encourage us. We follow him for many days, and grow accustomed to him appearing out of the sky and flying on ahead until at last, one day, he disappears over the horizon.

The next morning, we see the unmistakable contour of an island off our starboard bow. We have apparently drifted toward it during the night, though it is still far away. As we sail toward the island, there is a sense of timelessness, and of deep appreciation for this journey and for the albatross and dolphins and for everyone who, by touching us, has helped us and is with us now. Feedback. Awareness. The island looms closer.

We make landfall shortly before sunset near a beach that stretches out among some palm trees in the evening light. We set up camp, meditate, and before long we are fast asleep on the sandy shore under a warm moonlit sky. An unusually vivid dream arises in our mind, and in the dream we are transported to a beautiful garden in a valley by a small stream where we are sitting with a woman who communicates with us through her ageless eyes, and through a lilting voice we hear as if coming from within us.

"You have arrived here on the Island of Imagination; welcome! And while your body sleeps, we will learn, yes, we will learn. Not so many people find us way out here, beyond, but we are here, always here.

"Your imagination is a mighty power, and is meant to be your helper and your friend. Like any power, if you use her wrongly, though, she can destroy. She can be terrible too. Let her serve your highest dream and you may see she bears wisdom from the Other Shore.

"You are working to purify your heart, so your imagination is your friend. You can trust her to inspire, and to guide you on your way. She can open new doors of understanding. Deep messages may come in images from your inner wisdom. They may be seeds of new creations to uplift the world, intuitions to bring spirit more brightly into life. Imagination back on the shore you came from is mostly a distraction. The ox's tail, self-preoccupied, loves to use imagination and memory to reinforce its story: all its plans, wishes, regrets, fears, and complicated intrigues are bundled into its stream of wordy imaginings, and so imagination may often be a tool to further its delusion. It can be a way to ignore the presence of being all around you, and the poignant beauty of life as it is!

"You, though, have glimpsed the field of being, and are becoming more simple and undistracted again, and your imagination can serve the light of intuition. You seem ready to explore the power of imagination, to serve the creative spirit within you.

"There seem to be three primary domains of imagery, three related realms in imagination. The visual domain is most obvious: everything that you see or can see with your inner eye, representational and abstract. With closed eyes you can see the ocean waves breaking on this white beach, the palm trees in the wind, and the moonlight on the water, and it's all an inner vision, seen with your inner eye. Or now, see the kaleidoscope of colors whirling and swirling, and the play of light, dancing. Visual imagery is inner seeing, and comes easier when you close your eyes.

"A second domain of your imagination is auditory, hearing with your inner ear. Listen within; you can hear the sound of rolling thunder, the call of the crow, water in a stream, children at play, church bells. The possibilities again are endless.

"The third realm of imagination is kinesthetic, everything you can feel within. Feel yourself dancing now, leaping in great hoops, and rising off the Earth, soaring and floating, now turning over and around and landing again, and lying on your back in the warm sun; feel the warmth of the sun spreading over your skin and deeply into your body. Feel the tingling of energy moving within you, the grains of sand pressing into your back. This is all kinesthetic imagery, another boundless domain.

"Intuitive insights can arrive through these imagery pathways. For example, an intuition can come through an inner vision, perhaps in meditation, or as a flash of an image in your mind's eye that brings an understanding. It can also come as an auditory image, perhaps as an inner voice that you recognize as distinct from the usual voice of the ongoing inner monologue. And it can arrive through a kinesthetic image, such as a gut feeling, heart feeling, or tingling sensation. It's a good idea to get to know your intuitive imagery style, and if there are certain ways that images usually come to you to bring guidance and insight.

"We will now explore the power of your imagination to carry wisdom and messages from your intuition. Music has long been recognized for its spiritual power, and its ability to evoke imagery within. Four pieces of music are coming. As you listen to the first musical piece, allow it to evoke imagery within you and, after listening, take a few minutes to write down in words or in a poem or a sketch, just for yourself, what you experienced. It's like writing down a dream when waking. What did the music evoke, what inner visions, sounds, feelings, and sensations? Allow yourself to enter the experience of your imagination fully, and write down whatever arises. Then listen to the next piece and see what imagery is evoked within you and jot it down, and then on to the next, and then the last, taking a journey with the music through the richness of your inner seeing, hearing, and feeling. Let your imagination be completely free to play. Open, let go, and notice it all!

"We begin now: allow yourself to remember your highest aspiration and dedicate this process of awakening your imagination to

88

the benefit of all. Next, see what emerges in you when you hear this question: 'Right now, what is it that most calls out for deeper understanding? What is it that you would most like to understand more fully?' Something is evoked within you by this question. It may be a thought, a feeling, or an image; simply take note of it.

"Relax now and open to the music we will share with you, four pieces, one following the other with a short break between each piece for writing down your experience of imagination. Here is the first piece; listen, and allow the music to evoke imagery from within you."

The music begins and fills us, one piece after the other, each unique and creating a different response of images and feelings within us.

(For a sense of the four pieces of music from the Island of Imagination, and to try this practice, please listen to tracks five through eight on the accompanying album, *Islands of Light*. These four pieces comprise the four movements of "Fantasia in F Major," and they are: 1. "Vivace," track 5; 2. "Tempestoso," track 6; 3. "Pastorale," track 7; and 4. "Trionfale," track 8.)

"Now that you've listened to the four pieces of music and written down the images and feelings they evoked within you, allow yourself, in this unique inner space you're in, to write a poem. Even if you have never written a poem before, try it, in an effortless way. Just let your heart write and let the poem within you at this moment emerge onto the paper. It doesn't have to rhyme or have meter; just let it flow out of you, with no judgment or comparing. Let it simply become and be."

We try it and enjoy the sense of poetic creativity that the imagery experience has helped evoke. A poem slides out surprisingly easily onto our paper.

"You are experiencing the matrix of intuition, creativity, and spirituality. These three flow together and they can trigger each other through the power of your imagination. Your imagination has its own unique style. For example, is your imagery more visual, auditory, or kinesthetic? Is it more verbal or less verbal? Are you involved directly in the experiences of your imagination, or do you watch like an observer watching a movie? What deeper understandings have emerged as a result of this music and imagery experience? Can you apply these messages from your imagination practically in your daily life? Are they suggesting attitudes that you can adopt, or fresh perspectives on yourself or others? Do you recognize connections between your imagery experiences and the questions you are working with right now in your life?

"Please continue to work with any images that seem particularly suggestive or mysterious; they are beckoning and contain power and insight that may yet be eluding you. Your wise inner teacher, your intuitive wisdom, will use an opportunity like this to convey insight and guidance. It can be helpful to respect whatever imagery experiences you have received, and to work with the images within you by writing about them in a journal, meditating on them, sharing them, or letting them be the seeds for creative expressions in painting, poetry, story-writing, music, dance, or sculpture. In time, more facets to these jewels you have given yourself may be revealed.

"In many ways, your conscious mind is like a thin layer or veneer that you've been trained to rely on and to identify with as the sole power for making decisions and understanding your life. And yet, extending deep below this surface layer and far above it as well, like the sea and sky, are levels of consciousness that are available to you through meditation and imagination. Visual, kinesthetic, and auditory imagery experiences can carry healing and awakening power from these other levels. These experiences can convey complex understandings in relatively swift and simple images that are often symbolic. As you unpack the meanings contained within them, you will be fed the most nourishing food, awareness. Nurture this pathway within you—the pathway from the surface layer of your conscious mind to your intuitive heart—by honoring the fertile garden of metaphoric images you receive, contemplating and interpreting them, learning from them, and incorporating them into the fabric of your consciousness and daily life. They can transform you and enrich your life.

"And when you are at an impasse, either in your inner life or your outer world, if you persist in meditation, you will find that it is often an image that will suddenly break the impasse. As a gift from your higher wisdom, it can catapult you into another level, or integrate apparently conflicting aspects of yourself. Be watchful. Symbolic images appear all the time! There are seldom coincidences with these images. They originate from your inner wisdom, arising within and often in the outer world as well, as concrete perceptions. Outer events in your life and in the shared life of your culture, though they appear to be literal, can also be seen as symbolic, and as you learn to see this way, you may well find your intuition growing. You can begin to see the connections between your inner world and your experience of the outer world.

"When you dream at night or during a nap, or even during a daydream, you can experience the remarkable creativity of your imagination. You are finding that as your meditation practice develops, you are more aware in your dreams, and you can enjoy and benefit from the creative exuberance of your mind in dreaming.

"The messages that your intuitive wisdom delivers to you in dreams, and often at other times as well, are in the form of symbols in which characters, events, places, and things represent something else. Symbols are one of the main languages of the intuitive muse, and are central to the languages of myth, art, and scripture. Symbols are multidimensional and ambiguous, so the meanings are not contained in literal words but call to be interpreted, and symbol interpretation, while foreign to the literalist rational mind, is where the intuitive mind excels. As your intuition flowers, you may naturally begin to sense the hidden symbolic meanings in literature, in art, in spiritual teachings, in your dreams, and in your daily life.

"As you continue to the Other Shore, you may find your dreams becoming more helpful and inspiring as you bridge the gulf that separates the dreaming self and the waking self. These two selves can become allies for each other, mediated by your intuition's wisdom in interpreting symbols. You may begin to be aware you are dreaming when you're awake, and that you're awake when you're dreaming. You may begin to see realities more symbolically, as symbolic of inner processes and qualities, and your intuition will help you to see beyond surface levels to the underlying significance of the events of both your waking life and your dreams. This can be a key to intuitive living, encouraging your ability to see otherwise hidden connections and relationships.

"As your energy increases and as your meditation practice develops, your heart's aspirations may create a field that will evoke symbolic images to guide you on your path, both in your waking life as well as in your dreams. Perhaps nothing is by accident or at random. In many ways, the universe is conspiring to aid your evolution into truth. Cooperating with and being wakeful to inner and outer symbolic messages can help you avoid unnecessary suffering.

"This can be because messages from the universe, which is your inner wisdom, may need to get 'louder' and, from your point of view, more traumatic, in order to get your attention if you continually ignore them. Disease, conflicts, and tragedies may inevitably arise from being unable to connect with the wisdom that springs from intuition. Yet seeming tragedies often become, eventually, instigators of healing and awakening. What are they but your old friend, feedback? As you have already discovered, though, it can be far more enjoyable to work *with* the grand unfolding of consciousness than to resist it.

"It may become clearer how the inner and outer worlds are connected, and how the outer world manifests as an expression of the inner. What you imagine positively and clearly will tend to arise in your outer experience, and what you imagine negatively, and fear or repress, will also tend to arise in your experience. More than this, the experience you have of the outer world is, undeniably, an experience that arises in your own consciousness and is fundamentally unique to you, as your inner world is also unique. Becoming more sensitive to the direct connection between your outer experience of life and your thoughts and inner state of consciousness, you may see outer events less as happening *to* you and more as happening *from* you.

"As you begin to intuit the connections between inner events and outer events, you may become more effective in helping others, and less critical and judgmental. Understanding more clearly that the outer world arises in consciousness, you will naturally free yourself from the cultural belief that the outer world can damage you or fulfill you.

"We are not implying that suffering is not real, or to justify a complacent attitude toward the suffering of others. We can harm not only by acting but also by failing to act. It is in our responses to situations that we can demonstrate and develop our understanding. So we can do our best to live by these four realizations: that the outer world arises in consciousness; that all beings have the seed of awakened consciousness; that all situations are inherently workable because all waves are manifestations of the infinite ocean; and, finally, that efforts to help relieve the suffering of others are a vital and essential part of this workability.

"Without training in attentiveness and mindfulness, the mind tends to flit between past and future, continually verbalizing, judging, avoiding, and grasping, and manages to go for days, months, even years, without ever, even for a second, actually connecting with the vibrant immediacy of life. The flower is never actually seen, the bell not heard, the glance not fully appreciated, the moment never fully opened to.

"Back on the shore you left, this seems to be how many people live, in a distracted world that their conditioned thinking weaves and maintains. If it would but collapse for a few moments, what brightness and freshness might come rushing in! But the conditioned mind is strong and rarely allows anything to enter its world that is outside its capacity to categorize and explain.

"The mind senses this, of course. Unable to enter and savor the beauty and enchantment of life, the mind consequently craves experiences that modify consciousness to allow some relief from its frustrating sense of being disconnected from what is real. Through countless activities, many being addictive, the human mind continuously seeks to escape its limitations and to experience altered states of consciousness. It seems to be in our blood to yearn to awaken from the shallow conflicted dream of living in confusion about the essential spiritual questions.

"Your quest for the Other Shore may be a quest to fulfill this yearning, to touch the radiant pulsing heart of the present moment. As you have discovered, being in direct contact with the present moment is an 'altered state' that is liberating and enriching. There are no negative side effects either.

"With practice, you may dream inspiring and instructive dreams. Your intuitive wisdom may be able to use dreams to convey spiritual teachings and also provide practical ideas for creative projects and unsolved questions in your daily life. And if you would like inspiration or guidance about a specific problem or project in your life, you can clearly visualize the question or undertaking as you prepare to sleep, and ask for guidance about it. Planting the seed, you can then enter sleep with your mind open and receptive. You may find that your mind is a treasure store of brilliant and transforming ideas. These treasures are whispering. You can learn to hear! Your mind can become your great friend and ally.

"The world appears as a dream of mind to remind you that as you imagine the world, so it is, and as you imagine yourself, so you are as well. Can you dream a dream that will wake you from the dream?

"Let your visions dance as forms! Bring them into your world to bless humanity and every being. Images have the power to transform your consciousness and your culture as well. By connecting with images that carry messages of truth and inspiration, and sharing them with others, you can help create a more sane, just, and abundant world for all. Your world is a product of the images held in mind, both individually and collectively.

"Awakening is not a dry and stale affair, but a freeing within you of the highest creativity and aliveness. The canvas of your creativity is your life itself: with imagination, your heart can grow brighter and your world happier. Create! Imagine! Doors open within the universe with this word! Imagine! Imagine!"

The island dream woman's lilting voice fades, and with her deeply-felt words, "Imagine! Imagine!" resounding in us, and her sparkling eyes still shining inside us, we awaken to a soft morning with a gentle breeze on the beach.

Rising and stretching, refreshed and uplifted, we spend the day reflecting on our evocative dream while sauntering slowly around the island. The experience with the dream woman is still vivid, and we remember the imagery that was evoked by the four pieces of music. Pondering and writing about these experiences reveals more, and we can recognize symbolic links between our inner life and our outer experience, as she mentioned. In the evening, sitting on the beach, we practice meditation, and feel our consciousness expanding into an awareness of the interconnections that animate the relations in our life. Feedback, never ceasing, flows through it all.

The following day, on a walk through a valley south of the white sand beach, we find a wooden sign greeting us with the words, "Welcome to this Art Garden" written neatly upon it. Walking on, crossing a bridge over a little stream, we enter a garden of beautiful flowers with pathways leading to a covered portico where six large paintings are hanging as if on display. A sign there reads,

> *Like music, art can be a language of intuition. If you look deeply into these paintings, you may receive gifts from your inner splendor. While each painting is separate, they also include and build upon each other. Seeing with the eye of meditation, you may be able to draw out of each painting a message, a prompting, or a revelation that is unique to you now. Perhaps, as you behold the paintings with quiet and open awareness, you will find insights emerging within you. Seeing with your eye of intuition, maybe the paintings can spark an inner light. Then they are serving well....*

(For a sense of the six watercolor paintings displayed in the Art Garden, please refer to the color paintings available on the web at www.willtuttle.com/Paintings.pdf or on the tri-fold insert possibly included with this book. For a sense of the music that accompanies each of the paintings, please listen to tracks nine through fourteen, the six pieces that comprise the work entitled "Songs from an Art Garden" on *Islands Of Light*. The six pieces are: 1. "Lost Island," track 9; 2. "Emerging Jewel," track 10; 3. "Inner Doorway," track 11; 4. "Time Beyond Time," track 12; 5. "Interbeing," track 13; and 6. "The Arrival," track 14.)

As we go to the first painting and stand before it, we hear music that seems to be evoked by the painting. Time slows down as we behold the painting and give ourselves to the colors and images, and open to its presence. We can sense life energy radiating from the painting's surface into the open space, and into us as well, and feel both a sense of love and of urgency enlivening the painting. Letting go of the urge to analyze the painting, we open to it as if viewing an aspect of our inner being. Time passes and as we gaze in the meditative silence we have been practicing, the painting seems to emerge before us, becoming more alive, and triggering intuitions that arise as wordless awareness. We sense connections that seem to radiate in many directions. Time relaxes and the music helps us enter the painting more deeply. The music at times seems to come out of the painting. We continue exploring and opening to the art and music as they communicate their energy and message.

At a certain point we feel guided to go to the second painting and when we do, a second piece of music seems to be called forth by this painting. We practice this island's way of viewing the paintings, which is distinctly different from the way we were taught in college art appreciation classes. Seeing the paintings as catalysts to help reveal aspects of our being, and as emerging from within us, we consciously open to whatever is evoked in us by the painting. We eventually go on to the third painting with its unique music, and then to the fourth, wandering meditatively from one picture to the next, and allowing each one to bring forth something from within.

It seems we are beholding a beckoning inner world from multiple perspectives, with each painting providing new perspectives including the ones before. As we open to the art and music interweaving together, they seem non-personal, or perhaps transpersonal, as if they have emerged from the unique character of this Island of Imagination. Although our conventional thinking wonders who composed and created these paintings and musical compositions and what they were trying to convey through them, we smile, sensing that in beholding we are actually in many ways also creating, and that their meaning emerges primarily through our unique perception of them.

After the sixth picture, there is an area with comfortable chairs and cushions, and we sit quietly for a while, filled with the images, the music, and the intuitions that float like luminous interconnected galleries and hallways within us.

We see that through rhythm, color, symbol, form, and sound, meanings not reducible to words and concepts can be communicated and celebrated. Art and music seem to be universal languages of intuition. Attempting to translate these subtle languages into the concreteness of verbal linear thinking tends to reduce their evocative glimmerings into codifiable concepts, disconnecting us from their potency and purpose. Finally seeing this with more clarity, we practice *not* concretizing the insights into verbal thoughts.

With our developing imaginal mind, we realize that we can think without the usual verbal dialogue, and on this Island of Imagination, we see how freeing this can be. Creating space in our mind through the practice of meditative awareness, we now understand our latent intuitive power more directly. We see that it's possible to understand and think without words through feelings, images, and symbols that are never actually translated into the usual inner verbal commentary. This freedom from the barrage of linear word thinking is a relief! While verbal thinking certainly has a role to play, it can easily dominate the inner landscape like a noisy motor with no off switch. We realize how we have been habituated to an incessant stream of verbally mediated thoughts, like an inner sports commentator at a football game, interpreting, analyzing, and justifying every experience we have.

We seem to be regaining the ability we had as a child to think without words. It is the reawakening of an ancient memory of being aware before the arrival of words and the need for a name on everything. With practice, aided by our meditation practice, we see we can intercede the internal monologue, discovering a richer experience of music, of art, and of the natural world. Abiding in the openness of this island, we look through eyes that seem to see beyond surfaces. It is wordless awareness, but in words would be something like: in blossoms, decay, and in decay, blossoms. In acquiring, losing, and in losing, acquiring. In the sky, trees, and in the trees, sky. Everything contains everything else. Words are shadows pointing to light.

The experiences on this island seem to have begun to free and empower our imagination. Releasing the habitual inner verbalizings that can become thieves stealing away our present, we look out upon the garden. Fragrant blossoms dance in the breeze. Birds call among the trees and a stream lisps quietly over mossy stones. The beauty and inexpressible poignancy of being haunts us, embraces us, and quietly urges us. What is it that sees and hears? What is it that savors? What is *this*? We rest a long time with this wordless inquiry, this ancient question, and feel more layers peeling away.

Perhaps nothing is ever separate from anything.

We notice with time that the moon is shining in the cloudless sky, reflecting in all the little pools of the garden. It illuminates our walk back to our sleeping space on the beach.

Chapter 5

The Island of Relationship

We spend several more weeks on the Island of Imagination, practicing meditation and thinking in images rather than words, and receiving more instruction in our dreams. We find other gardens and galleries scattered around the island and continue exploring the power of imagination with the music and art we find in them. Through all this, we feel our imagery becoming more vivid as we sense a growing freedom from self-preoccupied thinking. We decide that for the rest of our time on this island we'll do our best to conduct an inner fast from compulsive thinking. The more we're able to fast in this way, witnessing inner thought and outer activity, the freer we feel.

We walk the island in gratitude and recognize a growing urge to continue our quest to the Other Shore. We begin to wonder how it would be if relationships were based on a more intuitive way of being. How would people live together without competition, for example, free from the domination of conditioned separateness, and open to their interconnectedness with each other and nature? We enjoy imagining such a world.

After loading our ship with the abundant supplies the island offers, we head off again toward the horizon. As we sail through the passing days, we find we're getting our guidance now completely from the ocean and the sky, and from our inner world. Over and over we adjust our course, relying on our connection with the horizon that joins the sea and sky. Each time we do so, it feels a bit like jumping into the unknown, adjusting until we feel our journey and direction aligning with the sea and sky.

As we continue on, our heart fills with a sense of reassurance and gratitude. It seems to take both discipline and trust to be guided by our kinship with the ocean and the sky. We move through them, embraced by their vastness, sensing our connection with the intelligence that permeates them, and that this same intelligence guides our voyage. Our hand turns the ship's wheel, relaxed and sure.

There is a sense that we're fulfilling a larger purpose with this journey. Maintaining an awareness of this makes it easier to notice when we move off course so we can adjust the wheel. Recognizing our old friend feedback, we sense the unity of our life and purpose with the wind, waves, sky, and sun, and with each moment. The key seems to be inner quietness so that we can be sensitive to guidance from the feedback we're receiving.

Continuing on for many days, eventually one morning we see what appears to be a rather lofty island far off in the distance. There is, again, a distinct brightness about the island, and we smile gratefully inside. We have been practicing the intuitive feedback dance at the wheel, staying tuned to the big picture and to the energy of the feedback from the sky and sea, and we have almost forgotten about reaching any particular destination. Yet, here it is! This remote island seems lost in the vastness of the ocean. It is delightful to physically see our destination now as we sail toward it, watching it grow larger as it emerges from the horizon. We smile, aware that we've been approaching it all along, and that our future has also been drawing us on, inexorably. Our spirits are high, soaring into the sky, and we can sense our bright old friend from the Island of Energy with us now, enjoying this moment with us.

We hear our friend telling us that this island is not reachable by those whose minds still struggle within the delusion of separateness, and who would therefore harm or commodify other living beings. It is protected. We feel both grateful and intensely curious as we approach it.

Landing in a rocky cove, we climb to the top of a hill and see that it's a fairly large island with several villages basking in the warm sun below us, radiating an aura of peace and happiness. We walk over to a shoulder of the hill that overlooks one of the villages and sit quietly. We begin to hear music that brings tears to our eyes. It is a timeless melody that swirls around us, coming from the air itself, and communicating with us a welcoming sense of love, tranquility, and transcendence. We are swept away by the music's haunting beauty, and as we listen, we begin to see people walking about in the village below us, and there is something about their relaxed and flowing movements that causes our heart to ache. Tears well up in our eyes as the music pulls and gently melts something within us. There seems to be a certain purity on this island, and we feel it working on us, stripping away resistance and opening our feelings. The music gradually diminishes, and we feel refreshed and uplifted.

(For a sense of the music we heard on the hill on the Island of Relationship, please listen to piece number fifteen, "Song of the Truth-Field," on the accompanying album, *Islands of Light*.)

Eventually we feel the shimmering presence of our old friend again, shining just in front of us. Opening our eyes, we sense a loving being smiling brightly at us.

"Welcome to the Island of Relationship! You have done well to reach here and, what is most important, we are delighted to see how much you are enjoying your journey. That really is the whole point, after all! As you've found, it gets better the further you go!"

Our friend continues:

"People here will welcome you warmly. They are glad that you've arrived safely. They have felt you coming for the past several days, and I've come to explain how they live. You will, of course, be free to visit with them.

"The people living on this island have been to the four islands you have visited. They understand intuition as a natural evolutionary potential and as an art that develops with practice. Because of this, they can allow their relationships to heighten their intuitive abilities, and their intuition to deepen their relationships. They do this first and foremost by the regular practice of meditation. The people here treasure inner silence and share meditation time with the children from an early age, so that entering into inner silence is understood as the natural process it is. Every day begins with people gathering to meditate and pray together. Group meditation is valued as a way of giving and receiving together, with the individual giving energy to the group and the group giving energy to the individual.

"It's clearly understood that when anyone enters inner silence, a healing field is generated, and that when two or more gather for this purpose, the power of this field expands exponentially, helping those in the group to go deeper than they would perhaps be able to alone. This field, because it is a manifestation of the truth of conscious unity and interconnectedness, is called the truth-field. Each individual contributes to the truth-field and is energized and supported by it, and everyone understands that keeping the truth-field clear, bright, and strong is essential to the health and vitality of the community. The people here endeavor to embody the understanding of interconnectedness imparted by the first island, and so there is an abundance of energy and consciousness. They understand by direct experience that the more they contribute, the more they receive. The truth-field connects them with each other and with the larger matrix of life.

"Most commonly, people meditate together as couples, families, and extended families, and as groups of friends and neighbors. There are also village-wide and island-wide meditations held regularly which everyone especially enjoys. Besides the group meditations, it's also assumed people will meditate on their own, and everyone honors the calling to engage in solitary meditative retreat time. Some go into nature for several days or weeks, or into hermitages that are scattered around the island, and some do this in their homes while maintaining a period of silence that people respect and support. The time that everyone spends daily in inner silent communion is the foundation for the relationships on this island. This time is not considered a duty or discipline because the benefits are well understood.

"Through the regular and ongoing practice of meditation, people experience the two foundational core values, individual freedom and social harmony, not as ideas to be believed in, but as universal principles to be awakened to, celebrated, and lived. Cultivating meditative awareness naturally encourages a sense of kinship with others, and a sense of freedom to fulfill one's destiny within this context of harmony with others. Rather than the old conflicted trade-off between self and society, or between freedom and social control, individual freedom and group harmony are seen, from the perspective of higher intuitive awareness, to support and fulfill each other.

"Besides meditating together, the people here love to do creative projects together, and while you can see the evidence of some of these projects, such as in the beautiful homes and gardens they've created, most of their creativity has disappeared without any tangible or visible trace, and yet it's still alive and contributes to the truth-field and to the vibration of love and inspiration here. Even on the shore you left, some people understand the transience of all manifest creations, and still sing, dance, and make music for hours with nothing afterward to show for it, or like the Tibetan monks, spend days creating intricately magnificent sand mandalas, and then wipe all the sand away when they're finally finished. People here understand that joy and life are found in the process of dancing with feedback far more than in any goals or products that result, and since their ego-tails are small, they crave no monuments or recognition, and are free of the delusion that they must build up a material civilization, earn a living, or impress anyone.

"There is an energy of profound cooperativeness permeating the relationships here. Competition is hardly comprehensible; it would only be found to be humorous. There are no games or enterprises where one must lose for another to win, and there are no judgings of creative expressions. And how the arts thrive here! You'll see for yourself when you visit the villages. Since the people's outer, material cravings are minimal due to their rewarding inner lives and loving relationships, there's more time for individual and group creativity, which is appreciated through concerts, exhibits, readings, productions, dances, and celebrations. And because they have opened their connection with their higher mind and keep it open through regular meditation, the people here naturally delight in creativity as a way of expressing beauty and appreciation. Their outer work flows from their inner work, and the music, art, and other creative expressions celebrate individual uniqueness and support the underlying social harmony.

"One of the most remarkable characteristics of relationships here is how telepathic they are. Most basic communication is done telepathically. People are comfortable being silent together, and have a sense of what others are feeling, thinking, and imagining. Words are spoken more for effect, as an art form, and played with.

People learn as children that they can never hide thoughts or feelings from others for long, if at all, and yet the whole atmosphere is so permeated with loving acceptance that children never feel the urge to conceal or lie. This reflects, of course, the culture into which they are born; adults here are aware of each other's thoughts and feelings and feel little guilt or pressure to perform or to conform. Their telepathic connection helps them be understanding and compassionate with each other. People are connected telepathically through the truth-field, and the inner work of meditation and prayer keeps the pathways in the truth-field open and bright. Everyone is vigilant to protect the integrity of the truth-field because it's so vital to everyone's welfare. You'll notice a deep sense of being at home here. This is due to the strong truth-field. People nourish it through their ongoing inner communion and by living lives that accord with the five precepts, naturally avoiding actions that would be harmful to others.

"An essential foundation for this is their eating. The food comes from gardens and orchards that are lovingly tended. The guilt and violence resulting from the use of animals for food has never polluted their bodies, thoughts, or actions, or damaged the island's truth-field. The importance of this can't be overstated. Because they eat only love in the form of delicious fruits, grains, nuts, and vegetables, people here don't have fear, grief, guilt, or violence in their blood. And because their relationships, creativity, and meditation practice are amply rewarding, they don't desire to consume things or substances.

"The relationships here are natural and loving. While it might appear that people live in a naive, pre-rational Edenic innocence, this is not the case. They are highly aware of human tendencies toward delusion and narrow self-preoccupation, and the greed, anger, and fear that these bring, and the suffering that's inevitably entailed. They realize that consciousness is primary in the universe, and that energy, matter, culture, and relationships all flow from this. This is the key to their elevation. By understanding this and practicing vigilance and attentiveness, the people here have become masters of consciousness. They do not dwell in the fundamental attitude of separateness and fear that is natural to the indoctrinated mind but dwell rather in the awareness of connectedness, loving-kindness, and freedom that is natural to the higher intuitive mind. They delight in showering appreciation and thankfulness on others. Bringing others happiness brings them the greatest happiness. Meditation sessions often consist of radiating purely benevolent and loving energy to every individual in the group and village, and to the plants, birds, and animals, and to the world and to the whole web of living Light.

"Their focus is on the inner world. They have developed an inner technology that is more potent in bringing happiness than any outer technology could be. As you have learned to avoid putting your hand into a stove's flame or walking into a tree, they have learned to avoid the inner contractions that lead to anger, criticism, jealousy, fear, and pride. As you've learned not to step off a curb into on-rushing traffic, they've learned not to hold harmful or judgmental thoughts about themselves or others. And as you've learned to lift your feet to go up stairs, they've learned to lift their thoughts up to higher awareness, giving thanks for and enjoying all the surprises of the day, even surprises about how they can improve themselves. As you've learned to respond to your name when called, they've learned to respond with kindness and see the best in others and to respect the dignity of other beings. They do this by cultivating conscious awareness, and by refraining from nurturing seeds of fear and negativity in their inner garden. Instead, they nurture seeds of truth.

"These seeds of truth are the understandings that emerge from practicing inner receptivity, connecting the apparently separate individual with the loving and eternal grace that is the abiding source of every being and every moment. People here understand the fundamental inviolability of their true nature, which is eternal and intemporal. Living this understanding together, their relationships are free of fear and aggression, understanding they can never get anything from any outside person that will complete or heal them. They understand that they are already complete and whole. Therefore forgiveness is rarely encountered here. People seldom lose touch with the truth sufficiently to feel they need to forgive another or themselves for anything. Forgiveness would only be called forth if people from a less conscious culture were to arrive and commit violations because of selfish delusions, and the forgiveness would be immediate and unconditional, coming from the heart of inner silence. Understanding *is* forgiveness. But it is unlikely that such people would ever appear here. Like water, consciousness seeks its own level.

"Through their meditations, the people here are in contact with many other dimensions of reality and with the beings who inhabit those dimensions, and so it would be difficult for an outsider to grasp or understand the richness of the inner lives of the people here. They understand that consciousness exists in many dimensions besides this physical Earth dimension, and they freely travel to and experience these dimensions. Quite often they travel to bring healing and understanding and thus to reduce suffering. They bring the same tenderness and respect to their relationships and lifestyle here that they bring to other dimensions of existence.

"Children are raised to understand and value their own uniqueness and potential, and have many loving mentors besides their biological parents. Because they experience little shame or fear, children here have very few knots in their psyches that must be untied in order for deep meditation to be successful and natural. They are appreciated for their freshness and energy, and for their communal contributions, as the elders are appreciated for their wisdom, patience, and experience.

"When a woman is getting close to the time of delivering a child, the custom here is that she meditates quietly under a tree until she hears within herself a melody that she feels is the unique melody of the being that is to be born soon, through her, into the community. She then shares this melody with everyone in the village, and those who are present at the birth all sing the melody to the baby as she or he comes into the world, as a loving welcome. Everyone in the community understands that they have their own unique melody and rhythm and harmonic resonance, and that each person as a unique melody contributes to the musical fabric of the community.

"Relationships on this island are outward expressions of the love that flows from the higher mind of intuitive wisdom. People relish the zest of collaborating on creative projects, and the poignancy of quietly walking in beauty together, and of helping each other reach higher levels of awareness. In these communal activities people demonstrate their understanding that their larger self is an aspect of the community's oneness. Here the vision of benevolence and generosity that characterizes relationships seems natural.

"A primary lesson offered by this island is the importance of personal spiritual practice. Without taming the mind and training it to be able to enter the silence, light, and intuitive understanding of deeper awareness, the joy and peace that people enjoy here wouldn't be possible. The untrained mind is deluded and naturally self-centered, destructive, and afraid. It identifies primarily with a physical body and with thoughts and emotions, and wrongly tries to use and gain advantage over others. This deluded and untamed mind believes it is a separate thing, and that its form, feelings, perceptions, and thoughts are its true nature. This wrong identification brings inevitable suffering. We see on this island that when people practice meditation and lovingkindness to the extent that they are able to extricate themselves from the illusion of separateness, they co-create a unified field of truth. This truth-field, a pervasive consciousness of lovingkindness, gives birth to and supports an enlightened society that is healthy and regenerating. Relationships here are seen as opportunities to create beauty and to radiate love into the truth-field, enriching the spiritual web of interconnectedness that is the invisible foundation of the visible communities you see here below you. Relationships are intensely honored and cared for here.

"Committed relationships are seen as effective vehicles for cultivating spiritual wisdom, because an intimate partner can reveal and mirror a person's hidden weaknesses and strengths. Within the context of the truth-field to which everyone contributes, and the commitment to daily meditation practice, these weaknesses and strengths can be explored, embellished, and transformed. While these committed relationships are naturally monogamous and are the vehicles for creating families here, they are by no means narrow. Partners allow their love for each other to radiate into the community, and to connect them with a whole tapestry of friendships. Their love becomes a function of the truth-field that supports the community, and all of creation, in an adventure of ongoing conscious evolution.

"On this island there is no higher value given to either the role of marriage or to celibacy in the meditative life. Both are seen as equally worthwhile pathways, and people choose one or the other, as they feel inwardly guided. Marriage allows the opportunity to work perhaps more deeply with lingering shadows in consciousness. Couples see themselves as spiritual allies and companions, helping each other to awaken, embrace, and integrate the inner dimensions of themselves. They enjoy the understanding and bonding afforded them by their commitment to share the life adventure together. Conscious couples also enjoy creating together, weaving and balancing their images and inspirations, and through this process of expressing and celebrating the complementary energies of the yin receptive and yang active forces, they give birth to new creations that are syntheses that neither person alone could create. The children born as the fruits of their creative urge are shared with the community not just as physical children, but also as music, art, poetry, dance, and celebration.

"Some people prefer to remain single and explore the opportunity this provides for more solitude. Such 'mavericks' can be especially free and effective as innovators, visionaries, and healers. The lives of single people are also woven intimately into the fabric of community life, functioning fully as family members, teachers, friends, and co-participants in the ongoing creativity of communal life.

"If ever there arises any shadow of interpersonal conflict, the people involved immediately see it as an opportunity to deepen inner understanding and practice. They give thanks for the opportunity, knowing that whatever arises in their consciousness and experience is a result of their own thinking, and make an effort to deepen their meditation to go beyond the delusion of self-separateness. They may also become aware that the community has joined them with friendly support. The community is sensitive via the truth-field, and automatically responds when any member faces a challenge. The individual is a part of the larger body, and any weakness in any individual is naturally understood to be of consequence for everyone. It is a joy to 'be there' steadfastly for others, because this springs from the higher awareness that the other *is* oneself. Although there are no rules at all on this island, there is the shared ethic, born of inner silence, that thoughts, words, and deeds arising from the inner truth-field are basically healthy, energizing, and loving, and that deepening the joy of intuitive wisdom through relationships and meditation is the real work to be done. Of course, it isn't work at all. It's the natural impulse to learn, grow, contribute, and create."

As we ponder the thoughts, feelings, and images conveyed to us, we feel an aching in our heart, and realize how deeply we have longed for such a human community and world of loving and aware relationships, and how hopelessly far away it had always seemed. It was hardly ever possible even to imagine it. Yet by steadfastly seeking the Other Shore, we have been guided here, to see for ourself a society devoted to living intuitively and awakening to the truth of the timeless teachings we have been receiving. Our heart is tugged within us as we look down upon the peaceful village below. We find tears from an old and deep place welling up within us again, as a sense of finally arriving home washes over us. Even from far away, we can see how beautiful these people are, how nobly they walk and gesture to each other, how upright and relaxed they are, how timeless and easy the sense of harmony among them.

The wise words from our childhood filter into us, "Seek ye first the Kingdom of God and his righteousness, and all these things shall be added unto you." We are honored to be allowed to witness this precious island and realize it's only possible because we have been somewhat purified by our quest for the Other Shore. Waves of gratitude arise within, and appreciation for these people who have undoubtedly persevered mightily to reach this more mature and gracious way of living and being. We keep thinking, "It *is* actually possible. It *is* possible!"

We see two people coming up the path toward us, smiling. "Yes, it is possible," one says, laughing warmly and welcoming us with an embrace. "With practice, anything is possible!" The two people, a man and a woman, are remarkably good-looking in their radiance. They seem practically ageless, and an inner light shines through their eyes and faces as they look lovingly at us. They're not talking now, but we feel them welcoming us and inviting us to re-

112

turn with them to their village. Together we walk down the hill and into a lush garden of flowering plants with streams and waterfalls and little bridges. We come to a sunny area behind a welcoming clay walled home with blossoming trees interspersing platforms, gardens, decks, swings, and benches. It is a fragrant, inspiring, and cozy place, and we begin a visit with these people that lasts for several weeks. We communicate at times by talking, but mostly in silence, passing images, thoughts, and feelings back and forth via the truth-field.

We learn that all we've been told about the people living on this island is accurate. The atmosphere is relaxed and yet intensely alive and vibrant. We can see clearly how intuition is essential to the quality of relationships here, and how relationships are essential to the practice of developing intuitive faculties. Relationships and intuition nurture each other, like the roots and branches of a tree. The telepathic connection among the people creates a natural field of understanding and empathy, providing freedom for everyone. We see that by developing intuition through the practices taught on the previous Islands of Light, the relationships of the people here are refined to a degree that far exceeds anything we've ever experienced. The love here is palpable and exhilarating.

We remember that back on the shore we left so long ago now, individual freedom and societal control were always locked in an uneasy and seemingly irreconcilable struggle, while here, individual freedoms and community harmony reinforce each other. Because people practice devotedly, their intuitive and telepathic connection with others leads to empathy and understanding of each other. While there are no outer rules here, the five precepts that we learned on the Island of Energy, based on cherishing and protecting others, are fundamental and are honored joyfully.

People understand that the welfare of the individual and the larger group are mutually interdependent. Because we are not solitary by nature, but social, we fulfill our purpose as we awaken and as we contribute meaningfully to our community. It is well understood here that no one can ever gain happiness or anything worthwhile if another is harmed by it. On this island it would be seen as comically absurd, like one finger harming or fighting with another finger for its own advantage. People see themselves as parts of something greater and find delight in cooperating and creating together. This something greater is not a corporation, a tribe, or a nation that competes with others, but is the family, community, and web of life that are all interdependent, cooperative, and mutually supporting.

It is fascinating to see how the people live, and how they relate to each other and to us. We also find it healing just to be in the energy field and example of such a community. Laughter and joy abound, and we are surprised at the high level of vitality we see, and the beauty in small details that overflows everywhere. Every part of the community seems to be an expression and a reflection of both mindfulness and love flowing through daily lives. Walking through the tenderly cared for gardens and orchards, we see this, in the homes and during the tasty meals, in the music and dance that punctuate both daily life and evening gatherings, in the artistic creations, and in the celebrations to which we are invited.

A spirit of social cooperation and harmony with nature seems to inspire their actions and attitudes. There is no money nor any need for markets since physical desires are few and everything is shared among the community. The concept of private property, an expression of separateness, is understood as delusory and unnecessary. Children aren't sequestered away in schools for education, but learn by contributing to and relating with the community. There is no need for laws, punishments, or a governmental system. The authoritarian relationships that characterize our old governmental, educational, religious, military, business, and family institutions are absent here. People delight in creating, in cooperating, and in resonating with each other and serving the interests of the community. There is no need for any type of coercion because interdependence follows naturally from intuitive consciousness. Conflicts and illnesses are subtle and rare, and seen as opportunities for growth and for deepening love and understanding.

Unlike the culture we have left behind us, in which there's a deep feeling of having been cast out of the Edenic garden, and a mentality of distrusting and controlling nature, animals, and the feminine, here we see a profound sense of enjoying, honoring, and caring for the precious garden, and for valuing animals and the sacred feminine. Through the truth-field, people here know how to contribute to and enjoy the garden as fully conscious cooperators.

We find that the children are fascinated with us, and that they like to speak with words a bit more than the adults who communicate more telepathically. One morning a child asks us, "Is it really true that where you come from people actually kill and eat animals, and steal their milk and eggs?" We realize on this island how incomprehensible this must seem to them, but we nod and say that nobody back there knows any better because everyone is taught in that way as a child, so it's inherited conditioning, passed on through the generations. An old man says to the children, "They don't know it, but that's the root of most of their problems."

We find that their relationships with animals are similar to their relationships with each other. There are no animals kept as pets or owned in any way. Articles of clothing, house wares, and other things never contain anything derived from animals. Animals are allowed complete freedom, and we see them everywhere: birds, fishes, lizards, frogs, monkeys, snakes, and many types of mammals abound. Because these free-living creatures have never been in any danger from the people, they have no fear of people. We begin to understand that animals live naturally in the truth-field, and that any aggressive behaviors toward humans are mainly the result of human violations of the truth-field.

How the people here love and enjoy all the animals! A favorite pastime here is to caress and play with the free-living animals, and to sit with them and commune together, sending and receiving impressions and understanding, as well as love and appreciation. Animals mingle and wander around, independent and yet fully related with and included in the community's sense of itself. The people delight in and respect the unique powers and abilities that every animal has, and because of this loving understanding, the animals rarely attack each other, but feed primarily from the plant life. We see that the people's communion with both plants and animals enriches their understanding and their lives.

At first, we are surprised to see that the level of technology is by our standards quite low, especially for such obviously intelligent, creative, and energetic people. With time, we see that this is a conscious choice and that more material technology would be unnecessary and damaging to the elegant simplicity of living here. Because their inner lives and relationships and creative outlets are so rich and satisfying, they feel little need for escapist types of outer stimulation. They have also developed a sophisticated inner technology, and have no desire for much of what our seemingly higher technology provides. Rather than a materialist technology that seeks power and control over nature, they enjoy fostering conscious technologies that deepen their connection with nature and with each other.

Through intuition, for example, the people here can communicate feelings, thoughts, and images with each other directly, even when they are by all appearances quite far away. Through their mastery of internal energy and their love of nature, they are easily able to be comfortable in a wide range of temperatures. Through meditation, they can consciously leave their physical bodies and travel in consciousness to many other places, both physical and nonphysical. If they need information, they are able to access inner and universal repositories of knowledge directly.

Because of their focus on developing their inner resources, the people on this island have little need to extract and exploit the resources of nature. They have absolutely no need or desire for computers, phones, air conditioners, entertainment devices, transportation machines, defense systems, and electrical gadgets devised to supposedly save time. Their lives are relaxed, fulfilling, adventurous, and filled with meaningful opportunities for expressing, growing, and relating. The inner refinement that is based on intuition supports this and is both the means and the fruit of their efforts. We realize that, materially, they indeed lack nothing, and the focus of their attention, while it includes the physical, naturally includes far more.

We see that the community has grown and evolved organically over time. Some people have homes in the cool forest; others prefer to be higher up and enjoy the dramatic views. After a while, people will often have an inclination to swap homes to enjoy a change. We realize also that the people here are quite sensuous, but in an expanded way. They delight in many sorts of sensations, it seems, and savor the various qualities of experience in a wide range of sensory phenomena. They enjoy the heat of the midday sun, and also the chill of a cool evening breeze, the feeling of dry rocks and leaves on their bare feet, and the liquid silence of diving into the pools of the island's cascading streams. Because they are open to life and without fear or inner contraction, they naturally tend to expand to embrace and include experiences and to savor them, rather than judging them and trying to avoid some while craving others.

We notice that a wide variety of races and ethnicities is represented, and that these differences are enjoyed and celebrated. Because everyone understands the fundamentally spiritual nature of all being, the different shapes, sizes, colors, and ages of people are seen as diversities to be treasured. People directly understand that everyone is essentially spiritual, so there is freedom from worrying about and judging by physical appearance. It's clear that no one is actually older, taller, heavier, or more wrinkled than anyone else because the essential nature of being is not material.

This intuitive understanding of the unity of all life with the source of being is also responsible to a large degree for the remarkable level of health that the people here enjoy. Disease and fatigue are practically unknown here because people are connected to the power of consciousness to heal, invigorate, and harmonize, and they understand that, through awakened consciousness, matter/energy can mirror the inexhaustible radiance and life of eternal being. The key to health is understanding the truth of being as consciousness. If anyone is challenged with an apparent illness, the community leaps to their aid with understanding that affirms this truth of being, and that comprehends that the individual is a harmonious manifestation of eternal life, regardless of the outer appearance. By focusing clearly on this truth, the apparent disease dissolves, like the untangling of a tangle in the truth-field, and this strengthens both the individual and the community, and deepens their understanding of the essentially non-material nature of life.

Needless to say, we discover that the people here live long, happy, productive, and enriching lives, free from fear, anger, and other manifestations of belief in separateness. We admire them greatly, for it is as if they have physically established the home of the Four Viharas we learned of on the Island of Meditation.

One evening we are invited to a group meditation, and have the opportunity to experience some of the community's inner life. Everyone is sitting in a circle in silence, and we join in. For quite a while we sit quietly with everyone, but don't notice anything happening. Slowly though, we feel our mind calming down and relaxing, and then we feel the presence of our bright old friend. Soon it is as if he is whispering to us.

"To join these folks a little more deeply, really let go of thinking!"

All our practice pays off now as we connect with the familiar sense of just being. The room begins to become brighter. We hear our old friend again, whispering.

"You're doing great. We'll just give you a little boost."

As soon as we hear this, we begin to feel our attention become more focused and absorbed, and our energy rising. Even though our eyes are closed, we see a beautiful green field emerging in our inner vision. Everyone in the group is in their own way present in this field, anticipating us, shining lovingly, and we feel them all congratulate us on our arrival and welcome us warmly.

We begin playing a game together. One person raises a glowing arm and we see what looks like a bird of light come out of her heart, and fly up to her hand. With a gesture, she releases the luminous bird and the bird flies to the hand of someone else, becoming a brilliant yellow. It is quite dazzling to watch the bird as she flies from one luminous person to another, changing color each time she lands to the most vibrant blues, greens, violets, and pinks. We notice that the tempo of her flights gradually increases. When the bird lands on our hand, there is a delightful sensation as she goes from lavender to radiant orange and flies off again. We get the distinct impression that this sensation is the love that she carried from the person who sent her to us, and she flies off with the gift of our love. More birds now begin to appear from others' hearts, each one a messenger of love, flying around and connecting the points of our circle. We are participating in a wondrous spectacle, as birds of all colors fly from hand to hand, spinning a tapestry of colorful light as they go, connecting us all with a love that grows increasingly intense. The woven light gets brighter as it becomes more complex.

At a certain point the intensity of the light and the love and joy we feel become almost overwhelming.

Multiple strands of light encompass, connect, and unify us, and from within this matrix of light the birds fly suddenly into the center and merge into one larger bird of vibrant white light. As this happens, we feel that we merge simultaneously with everyone in the circle. One radiant life lives through us, and though we appear separate, we are one light. The joy of this sings and dances through us. As we open to the unity we feel with everyone in this light web, our attention becomes centered on the brilliant bird. We feel ourself being elevated and purified by our unified consciousness through the strands of light, and we feel the group aspiration for compassion and healing increasing, with its locus in the bird's heart. As our aspiration to bless the world grows stronger, we seem to feed the bird and she expands, rising above us, larger and brighter. With powerful wings, she rises with mighty wing-beats, going up and beyond us, and her wings open a doorway into the sky above us. All of us follow the bird, pulled through a channel of light, and after traveling for perhaps several minutes at what seems like enormous speed, we emerge into a world of radiant light.

We are at the top of a hill of light, and around us are buildings of light, round and radiant. We see the beings who dwell here, noble and peaceful-looking, dressed in robes of light. They welcome us and sparkle with humor and joy, inviting us to make ourselves at home. We float around, silently exploring the wondrous beauty of this world of light. Pathways of colored light radiate among the buildings, and there are fountains and streams of shimmering light, cool to the touch, like water, with fish of many colors swimming in it. We have an intuitive sense of the fishes' joy. We notice trees and bushes of multicolored light, with flowers and fruits that shine jewel-like in what seems an endless display of color and beauty. Brightly colored birds fly about us and among the trees, sparkling and iridescent. Their sweet, joyful songs add another dimension to the aura of harmony and love permeating the luminous atmosphere. Everywhere we look, we see and feel beauty, peace, and the radiance of benevolent light. We long to linger here and simply soak it all in.

After a pleasing interval, the great bird flies over us, calling, and her wings again open a doorway. We feel ourselves pulled along with her, entering another channel, and soon we arrive in another world. We are again on a hill by a building, and around us are many beings, but they are suffering. It takes a few moments to adjust to the heavy vibrations of fear and loss here, but soon we see that we are in an impoverished country that is experiencing warfare. It becomes obvious that none of the people here can see us, and we begin immediately to move among them, sharing love, and seeing clearly that they are also beings of pure spirit who are certainly suffering yet who are ultimately unhurt by weapons or by loss of property or relatives. The scene is chaotic. We see men, women, and children hurrying to flee a group of armed men, and they seem to be completely oblivious to the love we are sending them, so intent are they on escaping. The armed men are equally oblivious as they chase the people.

Even though the sun is shining brightly, to us it seems quite dark, since thick gray and red clouds of horror, grief, and rage permeate the atmosphere. We can clearly see these emotional energy fields and thought-forms emerging from the warring people, coalescing, colliding, and in turn affecting the people and filling them with more grief, fear, and rage. We suddenly see a woman who, being fatally shot, falls and then emerges from her fallen body, leaving it behind like a dried husk. She rises radiantly from it and looks around, free and yet somewhat bewildered, and we send her love and reassurance. Now able to see us, she rises up toward us, and then, propelled by an inner urge, she moves off over us and disappears in the distance. We see all of our island friends praying and radiating the light of love and truth into this tragic drama, and busily assisting those who have left their bodies realize that they're not physical beings anymore, helping them leave the area and move on.

We can see that our lives are essentially a manifestation of consciousness, and that this consciousness transcends birth and death. Dying there, consciousness continues, and is born here. Dying here, it is born there. It has no gender, age, ethnicity, or physical characteristics. The significant consequentiality of thoughts, words, and actions is obvious to us, as is the way suffering arises from the delusion that life is merely material in nature. We also sense how this scene is a small part of a vastly larger picture and that it involves the consciousness of many others: people involved with corporations, governmental agencies, banks, military organizations, and weapons manufacturers, and that all are connected and caught up in an enormous web of delusion that they co-create together. The pain and suffering are certainly real in the drama we see enacted before us, and we feel our heart aching with empathy for these suffering beings. We also see that even in this dark scene, there are acts and feelings of love, courage, and caring, as people reach out to help each other, and some even willingly sacrifice themselves to save others. It is all profoundly poignant to watch.

Eventually, drifting away from the chaos, we float by some nearby farms. In contrast to the adults, who are unaware of us, we notice how the dogs, pigs, chickens, cows, and cats turn and look at us as we go by, and how some small children do as well. We open our heart to them and send love, and enjoy their immediate response, seeing and feeling their goodwill flowing toward us.

The great white bird spreads her wings over us, and we are pulled along with her, up into a spiraling funnel of light. We enter and seem to speed through it for a short time, until we emerge and see our body sitting on the floor of the meditation room with the others. Suddenly we're inside our body, relaxed and quite amazed at what we have just experienced. All of us look at each other and smile, acknowledging each other again. We feel a deep bond with the caring people of this community, and are grateful for the learning we have just received.

The next morning, as we sit on the beach contemplating and digesting our experience in the prior evening's group meditation, we realize that our old friend is suddenly with us again.

"Greetings! Is it not inspiring to realize that life cannot die, and that what we are, manifestations of eternal being, can never be essentially degraded or diminished or lose anything? As you are discovering, we have nothing and lack nothing, and we are never separate from the source of all appearances. All beings are related. We are all children of eternal life. You have gotten a sense of what happens when we remember this truth and strive to deepen our understanding of it, and also what happens when we forget it and make no effort to remember. Heaven and hell can be seen as states of being produced by the mind, and relationships are our mind's mirror. Relationships seem to basically reflect the qualities of our consciousness.

"It is beautiful to see your life becoming an expression of transpersonal love. Your life is not your own private affair anymore, as you can see. You are here to help heal and bless the world, and to be an instrument of the light that is in you. By awakening to the truth that you are, you are gradually gaining access to higher faculties. No one can see from the outside the treasure you are storing up in consciousness by endeavoring to live the teachings you've learned on these Lost Islands, and no one can take it away.

"Though it's painful to see such suffering, and while it cannot be ignored or coldly denied, you are learning also to look beyond it to the truth of being, and to be a force for healing and for uplifting others. What greater mission can there be than this? All beings are interrelated in the intelligence of universal consciousness. Persevere, and follow the highest calling within you, and when you lay aside the husk of your material form, you will have no regrets."

With this, our friend shines love to us and fades away. With gratitude, we savor these thoughts and this island's palpably beneficent truth-field. We stay for another few weeks on the island, learning more about the people, cultivating our understanding of them, and deepening our appreciation of their wisdom. We spend time communing and discussing, and taking more inner journeys with them to different realms of being. We long to remain here, relaxing, contributing, and learning. Our journey has been so long, it seems, and we recognize we could in fact stay here indefinitely. The people here have made us welcome, and we could meditate peacefully in this charming place, abundant with luscious fruits and foods, pleasant climate, and inspiring culture. Here it seems we are living in the culture of our future, which beckons and inspires and which, nevertheless, is still in our future.

Contemplating everything one afternoon, we let go of all thinking and enter the silence. We feel energy building as we remain in pure awareness, beyond thinking and imagining. A brightness grows, and with this, a sense of well-being and freedom. Just this! Every instant is delicious. We feel a strong wish that everyone in the world could know this reality, a wish to assuage suffering and to somehow offer to others a glimpse of what we have learned on these Islands of Light.

As we sit quietly and ponder all this, we see an inner vision. We see, as an all-embracing totality, the life of those on the shore we have long ago left behind. We see the cities, highways, and suburbs, the prisons and asylums, the slaughterhouses and battlefields, the factory farms, feedlots, slums, and starving children, the hospitals and the homeless. We see universities, churches, office buildings, mines, malls, factories, villages, and neighborhoods.

We see, feel, and hear the pollution and vexation, the desperate yearnings, the gigantic alterations of nature, the unending striving and conflicts—all like an enormous, churning, blind struggle in the hearts of the people, and yet we see, within all this, that there are also bright jewel-like sparklings. We treasure these sparklings and understand them as the heartfelt longings for equality, wisdom, and tenderness, and all the efforts made in these directions. These gleamings pulse amid the vexing struggle, and we feel them calling us. More strongly than ever now, we feel arising within us the strong urge to protect those who are suffering, and this urge lifts us, pulling us on toward the Other Shore. We yearn to fulfill this journey, and to share what we've learned. We understand now clearly. It is time to continue on to the next island, whatever it may be, in our quest for the Other Shore.

Opening our eyes, our heart is touched to see that about twenty of our friends from the village have joined us and are sitting quietly, aware of the significant choice we are making. Some birds, rabbits, squirrels, and other creatures have joined us as well, and we become aware of others on the island not with us physically but who are connected through the truth-field. It's a poignant moment, seeing how aware and caring they are, how they would enthusiastically support our choice to either stay or leave, and how with a certain humor they convey the truth of our connection, and how it transcends physical distance and time. Words dissolve and we resonate together in appreciation and heart-felt joy and love.

After spending several more days meditating, relaxing, and connecting more fully with our vision, we feel that it's time to venture onward. We say goodbye to our friends, sitting in silence together and listening in peace to flowing music that comes from within. The inner light brightens and we give thanks for these beautiful beings, and feel a family connection with them that is timeless and sacred.

Later, as we ponder all we've been shown on this Island of Relationship, we glimpse how pervasive the network of relations is, and how it embraces every seemingly discrete being in a multidimensional and inescapable web of relatedness. Again, we begin to hear music. As we do, we become conscious of our breathing, and through this, become more aware of our connection with every being who has breathed this air, and how the molecules that have played a part in the bodies of countless beings now join and contribute to our own body with every inhalation. With every exhalation, we become more consciously aware that we're releasing molecules from our body-mind that will be incorporated into the bodies of other beings. We suffuse our exhalations with loving energy to bless these countless beings as we allow ourselves to expand outwardly into the web, opening to an awareness of those who have contributed to our life. We realize that there has never lived a person or any creature whose life has not in some way touched ours through the vast network of interconnected relations.

The music we hear is the music of the infinite interrelatedness of life. In some traditions, the meditation on this truth of interbeing is referred to as the "jeweled-web" meditation. The universe is seen metaphorically as a vast net, and every thing or being or event is seen as a jewel, a node in this boundless web. However far removed, every jewel is connected to every other jewel throughout the web. All beings are genuinely related as a family that pervades time and space, with every event affecting every other event. Nothing is separate; everything is completely interconnected and interpenetrating in a way that rationality cannot fathom, but to which the higher knowing of intuition can awaken. And if one looks deeply into any one jewel, one can see, reflected in this unique jewel, all the other jewels of the web. If one looks deeply enough, each jewel contains the multiplicity; each contains the resplendent whole.

Looking out over the turquoise water, and beyond to the indigo, we allow the walls of conditioning in our mind to fall away again, and we open to comprehending the nature of fulfilling relationships as revealed by the example of this island, and by the music of the jeweled web that flows around us, every note unique yet enriched by, and enriching, every other note.

(To get a taste of this music, please listen to piece number sixteen, "Dance of the Jeweled Web," on the accompanying album, *Islands of Light*.)

Chapter 6

The Island of Compassion

Sailing on, away from the Island of Relationship, this beloved island, again we find tears rising. It is excruciating to leave our loving new friends and their remarkable communities, and yet we have a mission calling us onward. We're touched by how they all come out onto the beach to thank us for our visit, give us gifts they've made, and wave as our ship pulls away. Living with them has awakened us to a new awareness of the human potential for intuitive living. Though sure that our memory of our time with them will remain strong, we can't help wondering if we will ever return to this beautiful island again. We recall the wise words, "Seek ye first the Kingdom...and everything shall be added unto you." In consciousness, through meditation, they will live in our awareness, and we can visit them and take journeys together. Through the truth-field, we are connected.

Entering deeper water, the old exuberance returns. The horizon beckons, and our adventure calls us onward. The days pass as we practice our sailing meditation again, allowing the ocean and sky to guide our hand on the ship's wheel. We've been told there are six Islands of Light on the journey to the Other Shore, and that the last one, the sixth, is known as the Island of Compassion. As we journey on, we wonder how far away this last island is. Perhaps we can bypass it and sail all the way straight to the Other Shore!

We begin to notice many images of spirals. It starts in our dreams, and sometimes in meditation: various images of spirals spontaneously appear before us. We see circles becoming spirals as we rotate under them and see their depth. What might look like circling on the surface may actually be spiraling when seen from a deeper or higher perspective. We see spirals everywhere we look, in clouds, in water, and in the ropes and wood on our ship. Images of circles and spirals dance through our inner and outer worlds.

The long days allow us time to reflect on all we have learned from the five Islands of Light we've visited, and to feel how blessed we've been to find them. Meditating on deck in the early morning, sometimes we feel the shimmering presence of our teachers from the Island of Energy. Their loving support reminds us of the inherent joy we have discovered within us, which we feel permeating the world. We sense the jeweled web glimmering in our understanding, urging us beyond old habits of perception. Everything is connected.

As we continue, we begin to have a strange feeling of returning. It is unsettling at first, as we're still journeying toward the Other Shore, but the feeling grows with each passing day. Strong images of the shore we left so long ago sometimes spontaneously appear. Circles and spirals spin around us.

Finally we see land far off on the horizon and soon, as we approach, we see ships. It is true. We can see the familiar landmarks of the port city that we left when we set off to the Other Shore. Disappointment wells up within us, mixed with a strange gladness. We stop and sit quietly, going into the silence as we learned to do on the Island of Meditation. We sense again the familiar shimmering presence, and soon we can feel the loving atmosphere comforting us in our disappointment.

"Yes," we hear the gentle voice, "your journey has brought you full circle, or rather full spiral, and you are approaching once again the land of your people. The great continent they live on is an island also; it is the sixth and final island on your quest for the Other Shore, and is called the 'Lost Island of Compassion.' On this Island of Compassion all that you've learned can be deepened. You may find new ways to purify your practice and understanding. The fires of daily life here have an uncanny knack for exposing any impurities in the inner gold you've been discovering on your island pilgrimage, calling you to refine it further. When your mind is clear enough and your heart big enough, and your tail is small enough, you will certainly discover and enter upon the Other Shore. The way is through compassion for all that needs healing. The way is through this world. Although you would have liked, perhaps, to sail forever away from the strife and suffering on this island of your birth, in the end this island is the gateway to freedom and wisdom when you understand it correctly, as now perhaps you're capable of doing.

"You've realized that all of the Islands of Light exist as sacred instructional dreams, as mysterious arisings in matter-energy-consciousness—and this island is also such a sacred island. At the same time, the islands are all perfectly real: you are called to discover the truth of their reality and of their purpose, and of your own, and to realize finally the essential nature of reality. You have the tools and inner resources to embrace this island and its teachings, to bless the people here, and to be blessed by the light that shines through every being and every event here. Through them, you can reframe old problems as opportunities for healing the web through love and intuitive understanding.

"You don't have to try to remember all of these tools and resources. They are part of you now, as long as you continue practicing what you've learned. You are learning to incorporate them, refine them, and make them real in your life. The little plant that you've been carefully tending has grown to become a sturdy tree that may provide shelter, nurturance, and inspiration for many people. Don't be afraid to let the light within you shine into this Island of Compassion. It is sorely needed here. It is your purpose for being here!

"There may be strong forces of distraction and fear swirling at times about you; it's good to remember that you have now cultivated within yourself the keys to intuitive living. You've learned how to raise your energy, and you've practiced the art of entering samadhi, the sanctuary of awareness where the illusory walls of separateness fall away. You realize your intrinsic oneness with the source of life. From the practice of inner listening, you have developed your ability to live in mindfulness, bringing your full attention to every moment, to every action and feeling. You have experienced the increased joy, freedom, and awareness that are based on cultivating respect for others in the outer world and creative imagination and receptivity in the inner world.

"The compassion that you are alive to learn about and to express flows from this understanding. It's not merely about feeling sorry for others and fixing them as if they were broken, or helping them as if they were weaker than you. It is about realizing your essential relatedness with them, and serving them on a level they can appreciate while remembering and honoring the eternal spiritual essence of their true nature. You realize more deeply now that, while it is true that all suffering is but a dream from which every being will eventually awaken, it is nevertheless completely real to the consciousness experiencing it. By rejecting the cultural narrative that discounts the suffering of others, and instead making an effort to open to it, you can understand it and also more effectively relieve it. To bless others, we are called to work to liberate ourselves from delusion; and to liberate ourselves we work to bless others.

"Your intuition can be nourished and expanded by all this! The more you can see yourself in others, and others in yourself, the more automatically the five precepts will live within you, and the brighter and stronger your energy will be for bringing healing to this world. You will find the spiritual atmosphere is heavier and darker here on this Island of Compassion than on the other islands, so it will be helpful to practice meditation two and a half hours daily.

"This tithing of ten percent of your day can invigorate your intuitive guidance system, and help assure that the ship of your daily life stays on course toward the Other Shore. With time and practice, you may hear and glimpse the beckoning music and presence of the Other Shore. It is never far away. When you listen caringly to others, or to situations, or to your own heart, your intuition is nourished. As you feel your connection with others and with your source more vividly, your compassion will likely increase. This is the source of your urge to give, to bless, and to create. In these, lasting joy and peace abide.

"Your confidence in your life's direction, your ability to sense the thoughts and feelings of others, your sensitivity to the energy quality of situations, and your commitment to helping to heal the world can all grow on this challenging island. Your words, deeds, gestures, and projects all carry the imprint of your understanding and the brightness of your awareness. Eventually, you may slip through the gate, leaving the realm of the personal, and your inherent freedom will flow unhindered by habits of separateness. You'll be a clear vehicle for universal compassion and intelligence. As you learned on the Island of Understanding, intelligence is the ability to see connections, and intuition is the mother of all intelligence.

"Perhaps you will be able to practice what you have learned on your journey to the Islands of Light until you are practicing without practicing. As the tail of delusion disappears, intuition and compassion will radiate more easily and you'll be their instrument. Now is your golden opportunity to live more deeply than ever, to explore the wonders of yourself and this beautiful Earth, and dedicate every day to unfolding the highest within you for the benefit of all.

"It will be easy to be overwhelmed by the misery and brutality on this lost island, the aggressiveness and competition, the enormous delusion, and the armoring of the people. Their belief in the superiority of humans over nature leads to their thoughtless abuse of the beautiful island they dwell upon. The forces of ignorance appear powerful here, often controlling the media, government, business, education, and religion. These forces of ignorance are the result of actively ignoring the truth of interbeing, and they disappear as the light of being shines. The light of truth is irresistible and persistent. It is the future inexorably calling.

"It is possible to ignore and deny the truth of being for a long time, but not forever. The strength of the ego is actually quite limited. Please remember, within every heart the divine light seed shines. Please address that when you speak, and see that when you see anyone. As long as you are making progress in this journey that is your life, you are contributing. Whatever the outer difficulties may be, you can make an effort to transform those difficulties into deeper understanding. Please persevere in your meditation and in the five precepts; these are your foundation and lifeline. And if you should need us, call upon us. We are right here!

"Remember the ox! Only his tail keeps him from entering the field of freedom, the Other Shore. The Other Shore is discovered by living to serve, and entering into the present moment and abiding there. As you understand the mind's many cages, you can help others to freedom by your light. You are ready now. Go forth, share beauty and truth, whatever the cost, and you will reach the Other Shore! Remember, the Other Shore is as close as your own eyes and heart. In fact, you will find that you cannot actually reach the Other Shore. The 'you' trying to get there is the tail trying to get through the gate! Let the old tale go. The Other Shore is always right here. It is at hand. It is within you and is your true nature. We are with you!"

The force and love of these words act to trigger something within us. We feel another veil being pulled away as our vision brightens. We thank the wise old teacher, and survey the scene before us. The harbor is just ahead. As our ship approaches it, we hear music floating softly over the waves, poignantly speaking to us. Perhaps it is the music of an ancient memory, spiraling through time and catching us now as we return to our people transformed by the discoveries we've made on our voyage to the Islands of Light. Its source is unknown, and it seems to connect us with an intuitive understanding that our return is part of something greater, and that we will be making new connections and discoveries as our journey to the Other Shore continues on the Island of Compassion. We sense that our melody is part of a symphony, one note in a vast musical outpouring that we yearn to contribute to and understand. The music we hear reminds us of our roots here, and of our roots beyond this physical world.

(For a taste of the music we hear as we approach the harbor, please listen to piece number seventeen, "Song of Returning Home," on the accompanying album, *Islands of Light*.)

Entering the harbor, so familiar yet also new, we feel we are dreaming. Boats are speeding here and there, the precious air made noxious by their fumes. Along the jetty people stand holding fishing poles. The water sparkles and glistens under the sweet blue sky, and yet unwarranted suffering seems to spread over the land like a blanket. We see the water in turmoil before us, and yet we see the mighty ocean here as well and feel the power of compassion growing in our heart. Finally we dock our boat and walk into the town, like we're visiting from another world. What a spectacle! How busy everyone is! How hurried! We're struck by how pervasive and thick the societal indoctrination seems, how competitive the situation is, and how might makes right, leaving animals, children, lower classes, and future generations with little real protection from abuse and exploitation. Looking into this unnecessary suffering, we see people who don't comprehend the splendor of their being, and enslave themselves and each other, competing and oppressing, and sowing seeds of further delusion.

It is almost more than we can bear. At the same time, though, we sense that every situation is worthy of our loving attention. Looking out over the scenes before us, we see that, like all situations, they contain the seeds of awakening that can propel hearts toward understanding the truth of the interconnectedness and sacredness of all manifestations of life. We are grateful for this revelation in our seeing. It was always present in potential but was unawakened in us until we embarked from this harbor and followed our heart out across the ocean, seeking the Other Shore.

Our heart swells within us as we realize that we are home. This is where our work is, our opportunity to serve and awaken. We are freer now. We have nothing to prove, nothing to gain or to lose. We live now with just one purpose: to shine the light that radiates within our heart and in every being. This light is our source and our ever-present home. Though we simply smile gently outside, inside we soar with gladness. We've discovered our most precious resource, the intuition that reveals the hidden patterns of connectedness, and that awakens the compassion that was slumbering within.

The words of the saints and prophets seem to stir within us, and their meaning becomes clearer. We—and all beings—are eternally whole and complete, and this truth can never be undone. Our task is to open further to intuitive wisdom and act, think, and speak to the highest light in everyone, pointing the way toward freedom from inner delusion and from systems of oppression and toward the field of awakening.

The truth-field on this island seems to be hidden and overlaid by another powerful field, one of darkness, a fear-field. The fear-field is wide and deeply rooted and is fed, we sense, by the military-industrial-meat-medical-media-money complex, and by many of the cultural traditions that inform people's daily lives here. And yet, through it all, the truth-field abides and shimmers. We can sense here and there in the scene before us some sparklings among the people in certain gestures, and potentials in how they move and look. We smile again, recognizing the unstoppable radiance everywhere. Our heart yearns to bless everyone, and the more wounded and dark, the more to bless.

We realize how fortunate we have been to make the journey to the Islands of Light, and now to realize that This Shore of our origins is actually the Island of Compassion, the final island that leads directly to the Other Shore. We have been loved and protected enormously, and now our turn has come to love and protect in return, and to embody the understanding we have received by living it in our daily life here.

Our old life has dissolved and a new life is being born. Our journey continues as we live and work among the people of this enormous and complex island. Our journey is our practice. It is living the five precepts and it is living the liberation of interconnectedness. Our life is, as we learned on the Island of Meditation, to bring every thought, word, and deed into alignment with the understanding we recognize intuitively: we are not separate, and infinite life is our mother, and freedom our essence, eternally. Though words for the experience will pale, we see the ox standing in the gate walk nobly forward and enter the field of freedom. The sky brightens, birds sing, and trees wave in the morning breeze. Liberation for everyone is ultimately assured, and we do our work and play, whatever is called for, knowing this is so.

Entering again the life of this precious Island of Compassion, and embracing it as our journey to the Other Shore continues, we hear her enchanting music swirling through the space all around us, over the Earth, and across the countless ocean waves.

(For a trace of this music, please listen to piece number eighteen, "Song of the Caring Earth," on the accompanying album, *Islands of Light*.)

Epilogue

The Intuitive Imperative

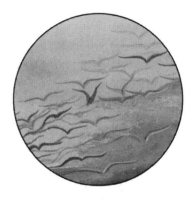

Pilgrims have been crossing the ocean waves to the Islands of Light for eons. This journey to truth is over pathless terrain; each of us is called to guide our ship toward the Other Shore, aided by our yearning and our intuition, and by our connection with the wise words and spirits of those who have gone before. It is the essential life-journey we all are on, though it seems well hidden for most of us within the distractions and urgencies of daily demands.

Consciously embarking on this adventure of self-discovery and cultivating intuition can be seen as more than optional luxuries reserved for the spiritually inclined few. It seems imperative for our culture and our species that we all launch our ship on this journey, because to evolve further, and to survive the destructive effects of our technological prowess, requires that we develop the higher understanding of intuition that perceives connections that our conditioned thinking fails to recognize.

In their quest for power, disconnected rationality and reductionist science have given us an apparent ability to control nature and animals and manipulate natural processes for our own benefit, but the price we pay for this one-sided approach is increasing alienation from nature, animals, and each other, and a deepening deterioration of our environment and of our ability to effectively solve the thorny problems we create. Without intuition's cognitive and transformative capacity that reveals the interconnectedness of life, our world becomes flat and self-centered, and we lose our connection with the sacred living web and with the inner roots of wisdom, compassion, and spiritual wholeness. We have become expert in taking things apart and separating ourselves from the natural order, and the intuitive imperative we feel is the healthy urge to develop our understanding of the interdependence of life.

In whatever we practice, we naturally become proficient. For many generations now we have practiced disconnecting from nature and disconnecting our feelings from our actions. The core of this practice has been at mealtimes when we have learned as children to disconnect our action of eating from our natural feelings of revulsion at eating the flesh and secretions of abused animals. As this disconnection has rippled through the centuries and through the fabric of our culture and all its institutions, we have created systems that multiply this disconnection, breeding competition and violence, commodifying people, animals, and living ecosystems, seeking to dominate and control, and imprisoning animals and ourselves in cages of iron and of fear.

How do we free ourselves and help others heal this disconnection, and unleash the latent potential within us for caring and joy? As with everything, the key seems to be practice. Intuition blossoms through the meditative practice of cultivating attentiveness, listening deeply and making connections, and our lives can provide us with abundant opportunities to develop our intuitive abilities. As we now understand, the inner dimension of this practice of making connections involves cultivating a mind of aware receptivity, and the outer dimension involves cultivating kindness and respect in our attitudes and behavior towards others. When we incorporate looking deeply, listening deeply, and feeling deeply into our relationships with others, we discover connections, and this can also nourish our intuitive intelligence. Intuition and compassion seem inseparable, and can help liberate us from self-preoccupation and from the delusion that beings are separate objects, or worse, mere commodities.

The race today seems to be between the violent destructiveness and despair inherent in thinking that is based on the standard model of separateness and materialism, and our ability to evolve a higher mentality based on intuition and cooperation. If we continue to emphasize, educate, and practice reductionist and self-centered attitudes, we may win some short-term benefits for those of privilege, but we may lose peace, justice, beauty, and meaning, not to mention ecosystems, health, and a viable future.

In making an effort to cultivate intuition, we are hearing the call of our evolution and of our thoroughgoing interconnectedness with life, and this call is the urge of the intuitive imperative. Only our tail of delusion separates us from the field of awakened consciousness. By practicing the ancient and timeless teachings of the Islands of Light, particularly the five precepts and the techniques of raising energy and the arts of meditation and creative imagination, we can learn to live more intuitively and contribute to building a more enlightened society that cares for everyone.

The intuitive imperative, urging us toward the Other Shore within, is the innate impetus of evolution. We are one life, and compassion is our true nature. This understanding can help purify our thinking and harmonize our actions, and as we awaken to this understanding, our inner voyage can continue, evolving and manifesting our outer world.

We may eventually realize that, being essentially inseparable from life, the spiritual and ethical evolution of all living beings depends upon us. We are called to nurture the higher understanding of intuition that lies within us like a seed. Every cell of our being is perhaps calling us toward this effort, right now and always.

However challenging our journey may appear to be, our heart's wisdom is always potentially available to inform and guide our life and fuel our practice, and assure the success of our journey. We are the ocean, yearning to receive all rivers, and we are the rivers, yearning to reach the ocean.

Words fade, and melodies, rhythms, and harmonies swirl on and on.

Final Blessing

Thank you, dear reader, for taking your interest in cultivating intuition and world healing seriously enough to read this far. May your efforts bear fruit to bring blessings of peace, freedom, and wisdom to you, your loved ones, and to all living beings!

Resources

Four Viharas Guided Meditation. CD by Will Tuttle. Meditation on loving-kindness, compassion, joy, and peace, for cultivating inner and outer harmony, with original piano music. 45 minutes.

Islands of Light. Companion CD album by Will Tuttle of original piano music.

World Peace Meditations – Eightfold Path for Awakening Hearts. CD by Will Tuttle. Eight guided meditations with original piano and flute, plus meditation passages from *The World Peace Diet.* 79 minutes.

The World Peace Diet. Book and audio book by Will Tuttle (Lantern Books, 2005/2016). Best-selling in-depth exploration of consequences of food choices, available in 16 languages.

Bursting Light: Favorite Original Piano Solos by Will Tuttle with Visionary Paintings by Madeleine Tuttle. Book of 15 solos with 25 paintings.

Daily VegInspiration: Jewels from The World Peace Diet. Book of excerpts by Dr. Will Tuttle with Zen brush paintings by Madeleine Tuttle.

Buddhism & Veganism: Essays Connecting Spiritual Awakening and Animal Liberation. Edited by Will Tuttle. (Vegan Publishers, 2018.). Essays by recognized authors.

Ascension; AnimalSongs; OceanPrayer; SkyHigh; The Call - Music CDs of original piano music by Will Tuttle. *Inspiration* and *Reflections* – Music CDs of original piano and flute music by Will & Madeleine Tuttle.

Circles of Compassion: Essays Connecting Issues of Justice. Edited by Will Tuttle. (Vegan Publishers, 2014). Essays by recognized authors on the interconnectedness of justice issues.

Conscious Eating: The Power of our Food Choices. DVD by Will Tuttle. Four video programs, including illustrated interview and lecture.

Living in Harmony with All Life. CD by Will Tuttle. Discourse covering the main ideas presented in *The World Peace Diet.* 75 minutes.

World Peace Diet Mastery and Facilitator Training Programs. Self-paced online training by Dr. Will Tuttle: worldpeacemastery.com

Intuitive Cooking. Vegan recipes by Madeleine Tuttle. Available at worldpeacediet.com.

YouTube video channel with Dr. Tuttle's lectures and interviews, as well as vegan kitchen and crafts videos by Madeleine Tuttle.

See worldpeacediet.com and/or willtuttle.com for information, ordering, downloading, other resources, and upcoming events. Audio recordings are also available through online commercial sources.

About the Author

Will Tuttle, Ph.D., is a visionary writer, speaker, and musician, and has presented and performed widely throughout North America and worldwide. He is devoted to helping people awaken their inner wisdom through education and to spreading uplifting original piano music through concerts and his critically-acclaimed albums. He is also the author of the international best-seller *The World Peace Diet* (Lantern Books, 2005, 2016), and editor of *Circles of Compassion* (Vegan Publishers, 2015). He has created a DVD, *Conscious Eating*, as well as three spoken audio CD's: *The Four Viharas Guided Meditation, World Peace Meditations,* and *Living in Harmony With All Life.*

Dr. Tuttle has taught over 20 different courses at the college level, including courses in mythology, philosophy, humanities, comparative religion, and creativity. His doctoral dissertation from the University of California, Berkeley, focused on educating intuition in adults and was nominated for the Best Dissertation Award in the Graduate School of Education. A Dharma Master in the Zen tradition, he has done intensive training in Korea, and has practiced meditation for over forty years, studying contemplative Christianity, Vajrayana Buddhism, and a variety of non-Western spiritual traditions.

He works with his life partner, Madeleine, a visionary artist from Switzerland, providing seminars, concerts, lectures, media presentations, meditation retreats, exhibits, and individualized music and art portraits. For more information about their projects, online courses, and upcoming events, please see www.worldpeacediet.com or www.willtuttle.com.

Made in the USA
Columbia, SC
24 March 2021

35003648R00080